What We Need To Face In American Education

WHAT WE NEED TO FACE
IN
AMERICAN EDUCATION

By Bill Madigan
and
Gary Kroesch

Edited by Mike Hogan

iUniverse, Inc.
Bloomington

What We Need To Face In American Education

iUniverse books may be ordered through booksellers or by contacting:

iUniverse
1663 Liberty Drive
Bloomington, IN 47403
www.iuniverse.com
1-800-Authors (1-800-288-4677)

Because of the dynamic nature of the Internet, any web addresses or links contained in this book may have changed since publication and may no longer be valid. The views expressed in this work are solely those of the author and do not necessarily reflect the views of the publisher, and the publisher hereby disclaims any responsibility for them.

Any people depicted in stock imagery provided by Thinkstock are models, and such images are being used for illustrative purposes only.

Certain stock imagery © Thinkstock.

ISBN: 978-1-4620-0366-2 (sc)
ISBN: 978-1-4620-0367-9 (ebk)

Printed in the United States of America

iUniverse rev. date: 03/17/2011

Table of Contents

Foreword

As I considered the honor and the difficulty of writing a forward to a book written by teachers who rank at the top among the thousands I have worked with in the last 30 years, I kept coming back to Billy Madigan — ably assisted by his supportive muse, Gary Kroesch -- in the other roles in which I have known them: as writers, fathers, brothers, friends, surfers, fishermen, wine connoisseurs, gourmands, jokesters, and especially as prodders and pokers of educational bureaucrats like myself. They are complicated and challenging people, humorous, sentimental, and well informed.

In the end, however, I am guessing that if Billy and Gary had to pick a designation for their tombstones, it would read simply and elegantly, "Teacher." And they would be so proud of that.

In the 21st Century and beyond, as we move - in the words of Daniel Pink - from the information age into the "outsourced automated" age, teaching will continue to be a daunting and rewarding profession. It has probably never been more challenging, as the data on teacher attrition from the profession tells us. But this should also be a time of optimism for the teaching profession, as we have more tools at our disposal than ever before and a national need that is compelling. This book is one of the best tools you will find.

I have often said that teaching was by far the best job I ever had, and nothing is more rewarding for us than to meet up with a former student and to hear from him or her that we did something that helped make meaning of the educational puzzle that is our school system. It is frightening how much they remember about what we said to them, how we behaved, and the example we set. Yet, it also seems today that teachers, as I once heard a colleague say, are "Swimming for the bottom," moving into colder, deeper, and darker waters. At the very bottom, they find themselves grappling with accountability systems that focus on rote memory, with administrators (yes, I was one) whose changing priorities and aspirations make teachers feel like they are indeed drowning, and with a perception that public education is to blame for many social ills.

Billy and Gary, who are paramount staff developers, curriculum writers, and much-in-demand public speakers, receive multiple rewards because they not only get to hear from former classroom students—"Madigan, they say, "you were crazy and I didn't quite get it, and now I know you were RIGHT!"—But also hear from many, many current teachers with whom they work all over the U.S., at both the secondary and postsecondary level. I have witnessed on many occasions the magic they work in their training sessions, forcing their colleagues to "think outside the box," but also to build a new box. They are always grounded in what we know works for students, but also understand how adults learn best.

Dr. David Conley has written brilliantly on how we prepare students for success beyond high school, so that they succeed in college and in their career path. He emphasizes content knowledge, academic behaviors, and cognitive strategies, among other concepts, as they keys to unlocking student potential. Billy and Gary understand that. But they also understand what our friend, the author Victor Villasenor told me about what a great teacher does. "Preparing students for college is fine," he said. "But the most important thing is to create a love for learning!"

On some days, I am certain this feels like an impossible task. However, at well-managed, inspired, and coherent schools, teachers' voices are encouraged, carefully considered, and affirmed. Spirited dialog among faculty is respected. And the development of our students takes center stage, as their voices are also heard and used to inform the work. Billy and Gary promote this on their own campuses. A colleague of mine, Mike Neece, who is one of our great leadership trainers, has said that our schools are perfectly designed for the results we are getting. But what are the results we really want and need, and how do we redesign our work to get better results? What are the results that our future demands?

Billy and Gary often say that our students have plenty of information, yet how do they make sense of it, and how do we assist their development and help them interpret the world? International measures such as the PISA test and national barometers such as NAEP tell us that our U.S. students are not keeping pace in their content skills, but more importantly, are also lagging in critical reasoning. On the PISA assessment of critical thinking, we once led the world and now rank in the mid-twenties against other industrialized nations. Our job is not to give them more information. They have plenty.

Billy Madigan, with help from Gary Kroesch, puts the burden on teachers to understand the world of their students, to recognize that they live in what some might call "The Information Overload Age." As Billy has often said to me, our students have everything at their fingertips—whether they are skyping, blogging, chatting, networking, downloading—but, without the guidance of teachers who recognize the moral imperative of their work, our young people will literally remain in the Dark Ages.

Together, Madigan and Kroesch have over 60 years of teaching experience. More importantly, they remain learners, constantly seeking out new insights about the world, the latest research on teaching. Countless times, I have received emails from Madigan (or Mad Dog, as I call him) telling me I needed to read the latest article in the Atlantic on how children develop their behavior patterns, or referring me to the work of Sir Michael Rutter, Daniel Pink, and countless others.

As you read this book, prepare to be inspired, but also prepare to be challenged. Prepare to do the best work of your life every day. That's what Billy and Gary expect. That's what they do.

Robert Gira,
AVID Executive Vice-President

INTRODUCTION

For the first time in human history, we are living in an age where the youth of our nation know more about society's cutting-edge tools than the adults charged with passing society's technical and cultural knowledge on to them. Most of our young people have far more facility with computer and telecommunications technology than our teaching corps – and, generally, that gap only widens as students travel from elementary school all the way to university and beyond.

Teens and young adults are thumb-typing at lightning speed, blogging, skyping, twittering and surfing YouTube on a regular basis. Television, the medium of today's adults, is fast being left behind in favor of the Internet. Small wonder. Instead of that well-documented wasteland of platitudes and cloying commercial messages, young people find that the Web is their entree to a fascinating new world – in a way and at a time they want. It's, literally, the whole world at their fingertips – or just the slice of it that suits each individual. It's not the same refried cop show/medical show/lawyer show that someone else has been broadcasting in that time slot since before they were born. The Internet is this incredibly vast, mostly uncontrolled, highly personal – and, yet, anonymous – landscape whose scope is so vast its depths will never be fully plumbed. You never have to cross the same river twice. Nothing in human history can compare to its power, variety or the speed with which it has become the dominant cultural medium. Virtually nonexistent in 1995, by 2000, it had permeated every aspect of our social and business lives.

How are we to respond? Our children can search any topic, watch any video, or order a bottle of single malt any time they want as long as they can type in a valid credit card number. Many are members of massive social networks -- some 4 million on Facebook alone – where innocents mingle with predators. There is absolutely nothing to prevent our young people from wandering into the less savory corners of the Web, and many of them do. They can have secret conversations and virtual liaisons with strangers across town or around the world. They also can tailor their world view to their liking, frequenting only those websites and online organizations that agree with their belief systems – be they religious, political or nihilistic.

But their sophistication with technology notwithstanding, most of our students are still children or teens whose mental and emotional development is, literally, stuck in the Dark Ages. As we will explore in later chapters, human physiology has not kept pace with new technology, and this presents new pitfalls, dangers and challenges for both our society and our young people who are quite simply "growing up too quickly."

It's a brave new -- and, often, dangerous -- world that today's youth must learn to navigate. Now, more than ever, they need educators to step up and teach them how to be critical thinkers able to discriminate between the true and the merely seductive, to see beyond the glossy veneer on harmful websites, harmful ideas and, sadly, harmful people in both the real and cyber worlds. We need to spend a little less time teaching students how to take standardized tests and a lot more time developing their critical faculties, so they will be able to solve life's problems, profit from challenging situations, and understand the increasingly complex world they must ken at an earlier and earlier age.

No matter how they want to be perceived, students are not fully formed adults with the necessary life experiences that seem to be a pre-requisite to wisdom. They are children with not-yet-fully formed mental and emotional faculties; and, no matter how mature their bodies may be, how hip and intelligent they may appear, they are still not-yet educated, not yet ready for a challenging world and, thus, ripe for victimization. Without a critical mind, how can we expect them to navigate the ever-expanding world that is being created at an ever-faster pace on the Web and in the classroom? We need to teach them how to cope; and that requires a new balance between standardization in education and literacy in problem-solving and creativity.

We who have this sacred charge must expand our repertoire beyond the minimum expected and even the ceiling imposed by an administrative framework that is – let's face it – stultifying. We must raise our game to a new level and achieve our goals in spite of the system. We can't allow the various educational labels and classifications to impede us – problem children, special needs and the rest of it. We must look past the labels and foster a new appreciation for the innate gifts and human potential of each child-learner. Each child with problems is an opportunity to make a difference in a young life.

We must combine the "hard" science of teaching with the "soft" art of educating, combining *what we do* with *who we are*. It's a difficult balance to achieve because of the human and organizational tendency to swing, pendulum-like, from one extreme to another. Introducing new ideas that break a mold can be a difficult and slow process. At the moment, education is bogged down in an obsessive-compulsive attachment to what is "measurable" and testable. Well, the world asks a great deal more of educators than what can be easily tested.

New approaches and new paradigms will be needed if we are to successfully engage students who are totally immersed in a world that developed long after most of us reached adulthood. There is a generation gap here. Even though we educators also utilize the Internet, we don't do it in the same way, visit the same sites, or have the same interests as our students. We aren't part of their texting cliques, and don't keep up with the twists and turns in their slang and cultural mores. We moved on from adolescence long ago; and, even though we may have memories of it, we are no longer immersed in its feelings and concerns. We don't "grok" it. Of course, we all like to think of ourselves as still youthful and hip. But everything is relative. We must face reality: we are neither young nor hip in the eyes of our students. We are very, very unhip and not to be let in on the secret. Those of you who have teen children will know what I am talking about without further explanation.

There are profound and far-reaching differences between cohorts, all cohorts – and there always has been. Most of us who are now adults never faced much of what today's students have to deal with – at least, not as early or on the same magnitude. One of my earliest teaching jobs many years ago really opened my eyes to these differences. I was just out of college and working as a recreation leader and coach at one of the city playgrounds. I was in my early 20s and certainly didn't feel over the hill. But, just a few days on the job, I can remember my amazement at what came out of the mouths of the fifth and sixth-graders who came to the playground after school. I thought I was young; I thought I was hip; I thought I was in touch with popular culture. But I can remember being absolutely shocked and dismayed at what these kids knew, what they thought about it, and especially what they weren't afraid to say about it in front of me.

That was pre-Internet and sexting on cell phones. I can remember thinking that I didn't want my future sons and daughters knowing what those kids knew. But of course, there is no longer any way to protect children from the world. They are dipped in it. All we can do as educators is to try to give them the mental tools and guidance that will help them deal with this terrible knowledge.

We educators have to be creators and innovators and become adept with new technology too. It's challenging: keeping up with the technologies that our children seem born to conquer. It will require us to learn how to blog, Twitter, edit videos, make online elements and become "native speakers" in new – and constantly changing -- forms of technological jargon. However, it's more involved than just transferring old ideas to new technological platforms. We should also take this time of adjustment to make our teaching methods more dynamic and responsive to the constantly changing needs of students in the new world. Beyond the obvious challenges of learning – or becoming adept in – new technologies and new ways of teaching, there are less obvious benefits that accrue when the teacher becomes the learner.

We will gain an increased appreciation for and closer connection to the very tasks we expect of our students. Since teachers will be struggling anew with learning new ways in the classroom, we will know, firsthand, the challenges and difficulty of learning, creating a feedback loop that will help us keep refining our approaches to different students. By sharing in the learning experience, we'll be in closer touch with students' needs and better able to motivate and inspire them. The teacher-student relationship will be more collaborative in nature since, let's face it, most children do know more about evolving technology than we educators do. That's just a fact.

This new world is evolving as we speak. We need to run faster just to keep up with it.

1

Education for a Changing World

"Come gather round people . . . come mothers and fathers throughout the land, Your old road is rapidly agin' . . . The order is rapidly fadin' for the Times they are A-Changin'"
-Bob Dylan

Bob was only half right. The world isn't just changing, but at a mad, mad pace -- one many times faster than the tempo of his iconic tune. We who live on it have to run to keep up.

If we could reduce the entire population of the world to a village of just 100 people and keep existing demographic ratios the same, the world would look like this:

Our village would have 60 Asians, 14 Africans, 12 Europeans, 8 Latin Americans, 5 from the U.S.A. and Canada and 1 from the South Pacific. Digging a little deeper:

*82 would be non-white and 18 white
*67 would be non-Christian and 33 would be Christian
*67 would be unable to read
*7 would have access to the Internet
*1 would be a college graduate

*5 would control 32% of the world's wealth -- all of them U.S. citizens
*50 would be malnourished

-Family Care Foundation

> ***"Let China sleep for when she awakes, the world will be sorry."***
> Napoleon Bonaparte

If we want all the benefits of power and influence that we have enjoyed for generations, we need to change. We need to accept that the organic evolution of nations now has challenged us to stand up and re-connect with our greatest attribute and national gift: ingenuity. The world and our classrooms within it are in great and ever-morphing upheaval, and our American character, drive and creativity MUST stand up and respond. We can avoid the rapid loss of influence and identity that Greece, Rome, France, Britain or Russia suffered (along with other great cultures) for one dynamic and remarkable reason: Technology and its synergy with human imagination.

We must do this in a new global reality, though. The world neighborhood is not the same. Considering the number of Asians in "our" village, it's worth noting that China has 3.1 million college graduates, and India has 3.3 million. That's about six times the million graduates in America's corner of the village. There is a huge pool of valuable human capital available in the East -- one that dwarfs that of the United States. Also, worth mentioning is the transformation taking place in China's schools and their emphasis on problem solving and creativity. Western countries should anticipate a growing Asian influence at the highest levels of technology, culture and economics, and find ways to make it mutually beneficial for all.

After all, those five U.S representatives to the world village aren't all Anglo males. America is a family of Latinos, African descendants, Asians, Native Americans and many others.

Consider the success rates of folks in our corner of the "village." Only 69% of America's high school students graduate. Of that total, 79% are Asian students and 76% are Anglo students. Only 57% Native Americans, 55% African Americans, and 53% Hispanics complete high school. Then, only 30% of those who enroll in college make it though their sophomore year, and less than 50% receive college degrees.

*In 35 of the largest cities in our "village," fewer that 50% of ninth graders finish high school. - **National High School Alliance statistics.***

While 31% of white and 27% of African American students drop out of high school, fully 56% of our Latino villagers have not progressed past the ninth grade.

Keep in mind that these numbers are in flux, and that our village identity is a moving target. Our world is in flux.

Turning to the largest cohort in our "village," we see great change in China, in particular. One of my friends, an entrepreneur named Richard, who recently returned from China, remarked that, "the Chinese are hungry." He speaks with wonder and in great detail about how much new construction and entrepreneurial risk-taking is taking place within China's borders and the surrounding emerging Asian economies. There are new companies, new alliances with Western enterprises, exponential growth in these countries' infrastructure, imports and exports and a remarkable increase in living standards and economic sophistication as a result. As developed economies, burdened with debt, face low population and economic growth, the explosive economies of the Pacific Rim are proving to be the engine of world economic growth.

The Chinese sun is rising and getting brighter by the day. Its power in international markets has grown exponentially in the last 30 years; and its influence at the United Nations is also growing. At this writing, they have just passed Japan to become the second largest economy in the world.

David Gergen, a senior political analyst for CNN who has also served as an adviser to four U.S. presidents, recently christened this economic milestone for China "the most important development of the era."

Just 10 years ago, China's economy ranked only sixth in the world. But recently, the Middle Kingdom surpassed the U.S. as the largest user of energy in the world, the surest and most reliable measure of economic expansion. At this writing, China owns $750 billion of America's debt, which continues to grow rapidly from the interest owed alone. Futurist Martin Jacques predicts that China will economically and diplomatically surpass the United States by 2025

With no foreign wars on the horizon for its People's Liberation Army, China reduced its forces during the 1980s, enabling it to redirect resources to economic development. With roughly 3 million people in five main service branches, China still fields the world's largest military force. When a modernized PLA is considered along with China's growing economic advantage, it is increasingly able to threaten America, not only economically, but also militarily. Can cultural influence be very far behind?

Even the lone developed, English-speaking nation in Asia is taking notice. Some in the Australian government have stopped referring to Australia as an Anglo outpost, and begun describing it as an Asian nation. Currently, Australia does 80% of its business with Asian countries and 15% with its Anglo cousins, the U.S and England. That's equally true of New Zealand. A friend of mine who recently toured New Zealand with his daughter came home convinced that New Zealand had become a colony of Singapore. With the clear rise in the economic, military and political power of China, India and the other Asian Tigers, America faces the most dynamic and powerful challenge to its economic hegemony in its history.

Much of the economic and educational data about America's competitors can be found in the YouTube video "Did You Know?" (The 2007 version is referenced here – the world changes so much, so fast, that statistics about the change are hard to solidify) But whenever I present this information to educators, many respond defensively. One teacher who was so upset about the raw implications of how fast the world was evolving, offered, "Wow, why haven't you killed yourself?" Americans don't want to hear it. After all, we've never had to deal with this level of competition in modern times.

We need to invigorate ourselves because the world is changing if we are to have any hope of maintaining our power, control and influence – both globally and at home. China, at this writing just surpassed us in making the fastest super-computer. We lost this position to Japan in 2002 then regained it with government funding in 2004. On the obvious level, we need to accept that China is running WITH us, now. On the more challenging level we must see that the race for the fastest computer by the best and brightest minds of China, Japan and the United States will only increase the speed of technological change in our lives.

Our national character understands how to stay ahead. What we must face now is that we have real competition. We emerged from World War II as the only major nation relatively unscathed, and have since enjoyed what I call "an easy acquiescence." We've had it made in all ways - without serious competition. We helped nurse Japan and Germany and the rest of Europe back to health and have been able to tell the rest of the world, "We're your daddy!"

Culturally we were worshipped; politically we were the envy of the whole world. I remember, as a child, seeing how people of varying nations and cultures had shrines in their homes with photos of John Kennedy. When Lyndon Johnson visited several Asian countries, thousands and thousands of people lined the roads, hundreds deep, to get a glimpse of his motorcade. We were not only powerful, we were perceived as the bearers of freedom and opportunity.

We were the primary model of high moral purpose. We were the big dog in the global neighborhood. But we aren't a Rottweiler or Pit Bull. We were more like Lassie rescuing the rest of the world after it fell down the mine shaft of WWII. At least, that's how we appeared. We have been living a dream, in part, resulting from two global wars that debilitated the competition just as we were hitting our "stride" socially, culturally, militarily, and economically.

WE were hungry. WE were getting our first radios, TVs, homes, cars, college degrees etc. When a people are free to realize dreams, to realize concrete material advancement through hard work, AND see themselves as top dog, they can go far. Personal and national pride combined with a clear increase in material wealth creates powerful motivation. We had the power individually and collectively that ONLY comes when history, industry, moral purpose and economic power combine to create a force of nature.

Unfortunately, as with other nations before us that achieved global reach -- Greece, Rome, Spain, Portugal and England to name a few -- an end to the halcyon days always seems to come. Success seems to breed complacence. Success creates a vague or overt arrogance that weakens the "hunger" that we once had and that we now see in countries like China, India, and even Brazil.

Are we becoming too complacent? Have we lost the energy we saw in the young, powerful and vital image of John F. Kennedy? He took us to the moon and wrote *Profiles in Courage*. Today, our youth idolizes the nihilistic chubby kids of *South Park* or *Bevis and Butthead*. Is America becoming a big lazy kid?

Yet, Americans exposed to this competition and change, which is without precedent in our few centuries of existence, need to face the fact of China's rise. If we do not, we will surrender the economic, philosophic, and cultural influence we are still enjoying today. This defensiveness usually comes in two major forms: "No Way" denial and an array of "What if" scenarios that would alone, or in combination, slow or stop China's sunrise. Denial is the most irrational and intractable, held by those for whom facts rarely affect their opinions. I will call them what W.B. Yeats called in his day "the worst" of the nation. The "what if" group's best argument is, "What if the Chinese collapse under their apparent rampant corruption?" or "What if they suffer a similar real estate or investment bubble because of their rapid economic rise?"

Both scenarios are real and possible sun-setters. Yet, the hunger they feel is what we need to watch. Hunger can overcome economic pitfalls. They have a powerful drive that results from many variables. They are truly running on all cylinders. This hunger will treat any setback as a bump in the road. Their new pride and growing influence are too intoxicating; and, in any eventuality, is more than just a bump in the road. They will adjust to it as if it were only a bump in the road precisely because of the hunger and momentum they are enjoying at this time.

So, what do we do? We do what great companies do and what great individuals do when faced with great challenge. "Corporate America" needs to try what the Ford Motor Company did just before, and during the economic collapse of 2007: face facts, clearly and honestly; re-visit and redefine their goals; set priorities; re-adjust structures and culture; and build a common moral purpose and vision.

Compare General Motors to Ford. General Motors had become too large, too diversified and unfocused. They had to be forced into reorganization and refocused externally. Have they learned their lesson? At this writing, the jury is still out. But consider this: have we in education become too much like General Motors? Do we have too many distractions and "programs" that just serve to distract us and dissipate our energies?

Mike Neece, a director of the National AVID Education non-profit corporation, asserts that "when we have more than two goals, we have NO goals."

Too many claims on our energy wear down the vitality and cohesion of a system or organization. Sir Ken Robinson, an educational philosopher, asks us to remove all distraction and clarify the debate by tearing down education as we know it to its essential elements: a teacher and a learner. He says we need to be able to see the issue clearly, without administrators, district offices, unions and all the myriad of distracters. Indeed, Robert Marzano author of more than 30 books, is widely known as an educational leader and researcher states that any positive reform in education requires that we tear down ALL of the structures and cultural elements of the "old" system, so we do not slide back into bad traditions because they are "what we know." Thomas Friedman, a three-time winner of the Pulitzer Prize and New York Times editorial columnist and Daniel Pink, author of *A Whole New Mind*, discussed this issue of global competition and American education recently:

PINK: Okay. Integration. Right-brain thinking. Getting signals first. What else should schools be thinking about?

FRIEDMAN: I've added something I got from my friend Ramalinga Raju from Satyam, the Indian company. We decided that the greatest economic competition in the world going forward is not going to be between countries and countries. And it's not going to be between companies and companies. The greatest economic competition going forward is going to be between you and your own imagination. Your ability to act on your imagination is going to be so decisive in driving your future and the standard of living in your country. So the school, the state, the country that empowers, nurtures, enables imagination among its students and citizens, that's who's going to be the winner.

Besides world competition, exponential changes and growth in technology is altering the whole world. Some small but significant facts first: many students in my Advanced Placement English Literature class - twelfth grade high school seniors - cannot read an analog watch or clock. They can't tell the time easily unless the clock hand is near the hour or the half hour. They don't have to. They have their phones. One day, as I was leaving the teachers office, four senior class students were sitting on a couch, inches from each other, not talking. They were texting each other and other friends. The average teen texts a hundred times a day! And that number is growing. I remember recently that I forgot the meaning of "laconic" in class. In seconds my students had the definition on their phones. They can talk, twitter, blog, set up and visit web sites, email, apply to college, apply for a job, read the news, join a hate group and victimize friends and enemies and so much more on their phones.

Children graduating from high school today will be retiring from their twelfth or more career/job by the year 2050. But if we look at the economic and cultural changes in just the last decade, we realize that we can't even predict what technology will hold for us in the next three years. Can you remember how you listened to music before the introduction of the Apple iPod in 2001? Do you still have the cell phone you used before Apple introduced its iPhone in 2007? You could argue that its year-old iPad is the biggest development in reading since Johannes Gutenberg's invention of movable type in 1441. These are rapid-fire game changers from a company once given up for dead.

Today's young adults will be finding jobs that do not even exist today -- some future evolution of virtual reality, no doubt -- and they will face problems that we can't even imagine today. How well are we preparing our young citizens for a world so malleable and in such upheaval?

I had a student who recently graduated and was a stellar writer. She was the school's newspaper editor. She applied to good journalism schools, was accepted and is now confused as to what she will do. Our school, mired in the "industrial standard of schooling" prepared her, lock step, for a journalism job. You know, like working on a newspaper, or *Newsweek* or *Time* or etc. Well, newspapers and all print media are on their last legs.

A few short years ago, *Newsweek* was a real force in politics and public opinion. It's now fading fast, and is projected to fade from newsstands in six years. *Time, Businessweek* and countless newspapers have faced a similar fate. So, in essence, we prepared her **symmetrically** for a world, which is no longer symmetrical. We trained her to be a custom buggy whip maker just as Henry Ford was perfecting the assembly line. She still has many options, of course -- but they all require multiple skill sets beyond writing, editing and researching.

I recently visited the blog of a writer from our local newspaper. On the top right of the blog was a request for donations! This writer, another probable victim of a high school that focused on a single linear skill, has had to learn to be a marketer and advertiser as well. This same asymmetrical divergence of skill sets required by the new digital world is affecting just about every other traditional vocation and profession.

Anything the left-brain can do - any type of linear sequential processing - can be done with fewer errors by computers. The rote/routine tasks done by doctors, lawyers, accountants, and mechanics can be accomplished by computer programs called "decision trees." Professionals beware! At this writing, there are expert programs that are 80% as accurate as doctors in diagnosing and prescribing remedies for our most common ailments. These programs are expected to achieve sufficient accuracy within five or 10 years to surpass the diagnoses of human doctors for the most common ailments doctors deal with every day in the out-patient environment.

Computers are far more objective and less expensive than human doctors. Already, computer software applications are being implemented across the U.S. in various medical groups and HMOs that monitor patient progress, medicines, and interventions. These programs even suggest to doctors various paths of treatment. With healthcare costs on center stage in America, even a doctor's ego will have to take a back seat to new microprocessor power. The only issue is will these computers be housed in the U.S. or will these jobs be outsourced to Asian and Indian data warehouses where electricity is cheaper?

Real change is overtaking the legal profession as well. An uncontested divorce 10 years ago was between $8,000 and $10,000. Now, you can buy the paperwork for an uncontested divorce on-line at Lawyer.com for $250.

Lawyers find themselves also having to be tech-savvy marketing geniuses and advertisers along with all that goes along with the traditional lawyer's challenges.

This diffusion of what was once linear, predictable, and stable is unstoppable. It's just part of life -- always has been really. Our ability to adapt is what has been critical to the dominance of the human race over the Animal Kingdom; and is a character trait Americans have traditionally had in abundance.

The need for flexibility and adaptability is important nowhere more than in the political sphere. The old "Big Three" syndicated news and established news outlets, both print and broadcast, held huge editorial power in defining what was known or worth knowing. They collectively decided what should be the sensible view of the world and what should not. Today, this common view is collapsing into blogs, twitter, and instant real time reporting by "common people." There is no central clearing house.

While this is great for giving voice to the common man -- democratizing opinion -- it also undermines the opinion-makers who used to unify this nation. Walter Cronkite is indeed dead. The grandfather who sensibly unified our understanding of the world is gone. More extreme views are readily available on your smart phone.

Extremist jihadists have benefited greatly by the Internet, so too have the nearly 1,000 hate groups in the U.S. identified by the Southern Poverty Law Center. The youngsters responsible for the Columbine High School massacre outside Denver, Colorado, used the Internet to research their methods and stoke their anger. They were able to plot over the Web; and only communicated with those who shared their twisted views. They chose their biases and commiserated with like-minded people online.

Some psychologists say that this group think becomes more and more hysterical and myopic as "other" voices and opinions are filtered out. Uncontested voices can become crazy, savage and blinded precisely because the sequestered realm of the Internet offers no debate, only an escalating and fearful certainty. This is the same certainty that fuels Islamic terror, or domestic terror like that perpetrated by Timothy McVeigh, mastermind of the Oklahoma City federal building bombing. Unchallenged, brainwashing can also result in the rigid, organized and efficient murder of six million Jews.

Socrates believed that each human had a view or vision of the world, a particular piece of the puzzle of reality; and that, for the health of the community and its collective vision, all voices must be heard. In the blogosphere, people are too often going to sites where they get validation and feel vindicated. The art of debate, like the Socratic method, is fading from public discourse. Truth may become a static imposition on reality. Truth will stop being a constantly renegotiated perception - renegotiated after new learning. Instead, perception will increasingly become the rigid imposition of dogma that is full of dangerous certainty.

Finally, we need to accept that America is no longer a WASP club. According to the PEW Research Center between the years of 2005 and 2050, whites will go from 67% of the population to 47%. Latinos will increase from 14% to 29%. A quarter of the freshman class at America's universities at this writing has, at least, one immigrant parent. In addition, most of our immigrants have more babies than Anglos do, so the effect can prove exponential as we slide into our future. A recent study of professional women in America found that the most academically advanced and economically stable were not choosing to have children. In addition, one international migrant either walks across the border or out of the airport every 37 seconds. This same immigrant phenomenon with the low native birth rate is occurring in Europe as well.

The world as a whole is also experiencing exponential population growth. In 1750, the earth's population reached 1 billion. 180 years later in the year 1930, we reached 2 billion. Only 40 years later in 1970, we crossed the 3 billion mark. In 1999, only 30 years after reaching 3 billion, we became a family of 4 billion. At this writing, Mother Earth supports more than 6,900,000 human beings, and we are increasing our numbers by 216,000 a day! That's a new major town every day. We have doubled the world's population in only 11 years. By 2050, it is projected that there will be well over 9 billion human beings living, most of them in squalid, ever-expanding shanty towns that ring major city centers.

Sanitation, health and infrastructure will be minimal or lacking completely. Pollution will be rife and an enormous increase in the use of coal and oil will fill our atmosphere with all the makings of a global warming nightmare. As Sir Ken Robinson warns in his book *The Element:*

"The last ice age ended ten thousand years ago. Geologists call the period since then the Holocene epoch. Some are calling the new geological period the Anthropocene age, from the Greek word for human, *anthropos*. They say the impact of human activity on the earth's geology and natural systems has created this new geologic era. The effects include the acidification of the oceans, new patterns of sediments, the erosion and corrosion of Earth's surface, and the extinction of many thousands of natural species of animals and plants. Scientists believe that this crisis is real, and that we have to do something profound within the next few generations if we are to avoid a catastrophe."

We have a great deal to face from the economic challenge from China and India, to a technological firestorm of change, to the flux and alteration of our own national character along with rapid population growth. However, humans have faced and overcome a great deal worse than this, going all the way back to their origins in Africa. The miracle of our brains will show the way just as our brains guided us eons ago as we ventured out from Olduvai Gorge and began our long diasporas across the globe.

For Further Exploration Chapter 1

What We Need to Face About How Our World is Changing

Publications:

Brockman, M. (2009). *What's next: dispatches on the future of science.* New York, NY: Vintage Books.
[This book is a collection of readings illustrating cutting edge scientific discoveries with projections of their effects on our future.]

Friedman, T.H. (2005). *The world is flat: a brief history of the twenty-first century.* New York, NY: Farrar, Straus and Giroux.
[The title is a metaphor for the world as a level playing field in terms of commerce, where competitors have an equal opportunity.]

Friedman, T.H. (2008). *Hot, flat, and crowded: why we need a green revolution and how it can renew America.* New York, NY: Farrar Straus and Giroux.
[This book proposes solutions to environmental and global challenges in order to "renew America."]

Pink, D. H. (2005). *A whole new mind: moving from the information age to the conceptual age.* Crows Nest, N.S.W: Allen & Unwin.
[This book illustrates the need to utilize the whole brain, especially the creative capacities.]

Robinson, K. (2009). *The element: how finding your passion changes everything.* New York City, NY: Penguin Group.
[The author demonstrates the need to discover our passions for our sake and the sake of mankind]

Smith, D. J. (2002). *If the world were a village: a book about a world's people.* Tonawanda, NY: Kids Can Press Ltd.
[This children's book explains world statistics in a "village" of 100 people.]

Web sites:

Advancement Via Individual Determination. (2010). *AVID- Decades of college dreams.* Retrieved from http://www.avid.org
[Their mission is to close the achievement gap by preparing ALL students for college readiness and success in a global society.]

Fisch, K., McLeod, S., & Brenman, J. (2008). *Did you know?.* Retrieved from http://www.youtube.com/watch?v=cL9Wu2kWwSY
["Did You Know" illustrates through contemporary data the rapid changes occurring because of technology.]

Parnership for 21st Century Skills. (2004). *The partnership for 21st century skills.* Retrieved from http://www.p21.org
[This site has "tools and resources to help the U.S. education system keep up."]

The George Lucas Educational Foundation. (2011). *K-12 education & learning innovations with proven strategies that work.* Retrieved from http://www.edutopia.org/

TED Conferences LLC. (2011). *TED: Ideas worth spreading.* Retrieved from http://www.ted.com/
[This site has "ideas worth spreading – riveting talks by remarkable people on global issues in science, entertainment, technology, education.]

United States Census Bureau. (2011). *Census bureau home page.* Retrieved from http://www.census.gov/
[This contains statistics about our world.]

WordPress. (2011). *Sir Ken Robinson.* Retrieved from http://sirkenrobinson.com/skr/
[This site contains short videos of Robinson's talks on education and finding passion in life.]

2

Need to Know: Brain and Learning

We can't solve problems by using the same kind of thinking we used when we created them.

The true sign of intelligence is not knowledge but imagination.

Logic will get you from A to B. Imagination will take you everywhere.
                                                    - Albert Einstein, 1926

There has been an ever-growing river of brain-based learning over the past 15 years, and even though this river has now nearly reached flood stage, we as educators need to sift through this deluge in order to boost our understanding of how our brains learn best.

Amid this torrent we are discovering that the most important "neuro" news for us in education is that extreme anxiety and fear shut off learning, AND that the process of remembering or learning is best accomplished by integrating our emotions or feelings with the new subject matter.

That certainly isn't the Western educational tradition, but today we are beginning to understand how a holistic approach can enhance education. In that regard, it helps to understand how the human brain works. So let's explore.

First, we'll look at a basic structure of the human brain – how it has evolved, where learning occurs, and how learning can sometimes be blocked and even erased by painful memories. Then, we'll examine how the two hemispheres of the brain are involved, why they exist, what each does, and how they share and interact with one another. Next, we'll examine the latest thinking that supports the best whole person/whole brain approach to making our schools perform at a much higher level.

It's important to recognize that there's a psychological dimension that's always present in the classroom. Although we try to minimize the messiness that comes with the emotions and feelings, and try to ignore them through the use of mores and strictures, students are only human. They don't leave their problems at home; and there is significant evidence that many of the problems in school and hurdles to education arise out of various forms of depression -- both latent and mild -- as well as acute and painful emotional states.

In fact, the emotional dimension applies to EVERYONE on campus, not just the students. Teachers are human too! That doesn't have to be a bad thing. People aren't one-dimensional; they don't assimilate information in only one way. By being aware of all the avenues that lead to learning, we can make education a more pleasant and memorable experience. We'll explore the "whole person" approach to classroom learning, with tips and illustrations of new learning methods.

The Three-Part Brain

Take a moment and recall a time when you saw someone "lose it." This scene might have involved a student, an adult, a family member or yourself. Things were thrown; doors were slammed; very mean or hurtful things might have been said. Perhaps, the very meanest things were said and the most precious emotional taboos broken.

Call up, if you can, a mental YouTube video of the event and re-run it in your mind's movie theater. If you were able to do this successfully, you may have actually experienced some very uncomfortable feelings. Don't worry; that's normal. Strong emotions have a greater impact on our unconscious minds than we realize and often resonate with us long after the event has faded from our conscious minds.

There's another, more mundane, example that illustrates the irrational power of this phenomenon. Who among us doesn't remember those tug-of-will sessions at the dinner table when we were young? We resolutely refused to eat our peas or broccoli or Brussels sprouts, much to the chagrin of conscientious parents who were just trying to get something other than Coke and Snickers Bars into us. What seemed like so trivial a topic and irrational resistance to the rational adult mind has often resulted in a powerful emotive implant in the child.

How many adults do you know who, not only haven't touched a Brussels sprout in decades, but also regale anyone who will listen with tales of their childhood trauma at the hands of autocratic parents. Relatively trivial incidents can color childhood memories out of all proportion to their real significance in the grand scheme. But the emotional isn't rational. What can seem ridiculous and trivial to the unaffected, can be very real to those who experience it – especially, to the impressionable child whose faculties are still undeveloped and who just don't have a grasp of the grand scheme.

That discomfort you feel when you watch your mental YouTube video could just be a residual emotive "echo" of a similar experience of your own. We like to think of ourselves as rational beings always in control of our emotions – in no small part because society levies such heavy penalties on those who lose control. But the fact of the matter is that there are feelings over which we really haven't much control or even understand. Many were planted firmly in our unconscious minds by some event now forgotten that had strong emotions connected to it. This taps a very deep part of the brain, the autonomic part developed over many generations of humans going back to the days when we were food for sabre-toothed tigers and just about everything else that walked or crawled over the Earth. It's a defense mechanism reinforced in the DNA of generations untold: a deep memory of how unpleasant it is to be eaten. It sends just one irrepressible message: Run! Now! Fire is hot! Pull your hand back! Now!

On the other hand, since emotion is such a powerful component of how we humans learn valuable lessons – like fire burns and bees sting -- since an event's emotional content is part of the reason we remember it, that suggests that there may be some learning modalities traditional education has yet to tap. Perhaps, we can find a way to integrate this aspect of memory to help students retain knowledge by attaching learning to positive emotional events.

Emotion-packed events are going to happen at school whether or not we learn to profit from them. The "losing it" metaphor is apt. When we "lose it," we actually do lose several neurological functions, and this "losing it" illustrates what is called the Triune Brain. Basically, the human brain is made up of three interrelated-but-separate systems. Neurologists identify them as the reptilian, the mammalian, and the neo cortex sections of the brain. (See illustration below)

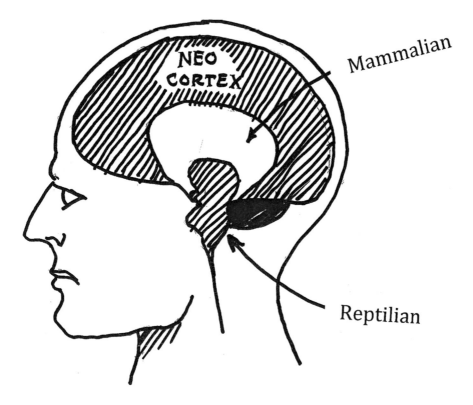

Meet Godzilla

The reptilian brain is the most ancient aspect of the brain in evolutionary terms; and, appropriately, it controls our bodies' most primitive functions. Made up of much of what we call the limbic system, it is a ring of interconnected structures along the midline of the brain and situated around the hypothalamus. It is, specifically, involved with emotion and memory and with our homeostatic regulatory systems that we don't need to think about like blood flow and breathing.

In layman's terms, this area of the brain, located right smack dab in the center of our heads controls functions I mnemonically refer to as the five Fs. They are *flight, freezing, fight, feeding* and -- well, the other *"F" word* -- which we in academia politely refer to as concupiscence or sex. When the reptilian brain is "in charge," it is the focus of robust electrical activity and increased blood flow to certain parts of the limbic system. In fact, it can completely shut off or put to sleep the social and thinking parts of the brain. A chemical "switch" is thrown and the reptilian takes charge of cerebral activity.

"Flight," the first of our five "Fs," is the primal fear response. In brief, we will run away from a perceived danger without thinking. If you Google any of the YouTube videos of frightened crowds stampeding in sports stadiums, you can see the rapidity with which people respond without thoughtful deliberation -- and, often, with tragic consequences. But this isn't cowardice or panic – as it's so often referred to in the press. It's a necessary and valuable response in all animals – again, created over evolutionary generations untold. If the gazelle to your right suddenly bolts, you better bolt too without stopping to check if there's really a lion in the bushes. Gazelles that don't move quickly get referred to as dinner.

It also happens to us individually and is virtually beyond our control. Remember your childhood encounters with spiders and snakes? I remember lying on the floor of my parents' house watching TV one night. We lived in a rural area at the time; and, I remember, just getting a glimpse out of the corner of my eye of a small king snake about the length and width of a pencil. I levitated! I was on the other side of the room by some unconscious combination of leg and arm movements. It all happened without conscious deliberation. Even though the snake turned out to be ridiculously harmless, my reptilian brain didn't stop to think about it. Hey, it could have just as easily been a rattler.

The primitive brain doesn't want to take the time to assess and differentiate among different levels of danger. That apparently is a good thing because thinking might slow us down that critical half second when quick twitch muscle reactions are precisely what we need to escape the clutches of some monster. They also may be all that can save us during an earthquake or car crash or the approach of a sharp object toward the eye. There are times when quick action is precisely what is called for – no matter how silly it makes us look.

Closely related to the *Flight* response in the Reptilian brain is the second "F" or "*Freezing*." When frightened, our bodies will often freeze in place – again, without conscious deliberation and, often, even beyond our control. This is an ancient and, apparently, useful defensive strategy that harkens back to certain types of now, hopefully, non-existent threats -- a charging rhinoceros (they're blind), and some types of bears and prehistoric predators going back to the last Ice Age. Its evolutionary origins actually pre-date our Australopithecines and, even, our simian ancestors; and you've probably witnessed the identical response mechanism in some bird species, small mammals and, of course, lizards.

Freezing may seem like an antiquated response in us, but some of these primal responses manifest in seemingly unrelated ways. I can remember when my grandmother died. We were very close when I was young, but work had taken me far away as a young adult and I hadn't seen her much. I was out of town when I got the news of her death and, being filled with my young self as young people are and my day-to-day pressures, it didn't have much of an impact on me. I was distracted. I just processed it and moved on to what I had to do to return to San Diego.

I returned to town on the appointed day and arrived at the church alone not thinking about much more than my busy schedule. But the minute I walked through the door and saw my grandmother on the altar I broke down completely and cried uncontrollably without let up for the next hour and a half. I wanted to flee the embarrassing scene, but couldn't move. I couldn't get up out of my chair in the front row. I had to be walked out when it was all over, and it took a long time for me to regain control. I looked ridiculous.

This is totally unlike me; and certainly not the image I want to convey. I grew up tolerating pain, never showing weakness and fighting though any challenge. I have no idea where this comes from or what to do about it; but, to this day, I'll start crying if somebody plays America The Beautiful or if there's a news story on TV about a child being hurt – a child I don't even know. I have to immediately change the channel.

Freezing certainly seems like an odd defense mechanism. It's not necessarily recommended as a tactic with tigers, dogs and armed men or women. They will not be fooled by this technique. In fact, police recommend that, when faced with an armed assailant, the best tactic is to run like hell, zigzagging as fast as you can. Generally, police say that the likelihood that you are running from a sharp shooter is very low and that this will likely save your life. Standing frozen makes you an easy target of even the most drug-impaired miscreant. Some of our primitive brain's responses are, well, just too primitive – and, maybe, out of date. But that doesn't mean they are not in effect, especially among your people.

The armed forces are evidence that training can overcome our most primitive responses. They specialize in the next "F" -- the **Fight** impulse. Experts say that roughly 93% of us will react to confrontation with fear, running away from a snake or other threat. The other 7% will actually engage the threat by fighting it. So, if you and I are in a hotel ballroom with 100 people and Al Qaeda suddenly bursts into the room, 90 of us will head for the exits, looking back only to shout encouragement to our seven or eight comrades who are fighting to enable our escape.

All of this is pre-programmed and well beyond our conscious control. It is difficult to predict how each of us will react to a given situation. Again, to turn to another unpleasant school example, what was it that prompted two construction workers to tackle the armed intruder who was recklessly firing a .357 Magnum around a North County San Diego playground in October 2010? None of those elementary schoolchildren were their own children; they were simply working nearby. Two of the children already had suffered superficial wounds; and, in order to save them, these two heroes had to charge the offender across open ground in directly in the path of the rounds he was firing. No one can predict how they will react in these situations. The response is something that comes from an area beneath consciousness – and, even, out of our control.

Feeding is our next unconscious control response from the primitive brain. Although hard to accept, most of us will kill to get food when hungry enough. Even the United Nations and other major aide groups as well as the United States aide agencies will strategize as to how best to deliver aide so that fewer people die or become injured by hungry mobs of starving humans. Trucks laden with bags of rice or wheat are often surrounded by U.N. Soldiers or local police regiments to maintain order. If the groups of needy people are large, helicopters or cargo planes drop aid across large swaths of territory so as to minimize excessively large groups of hungry people massing and rioting in one small area. We humans will lose conscious control of our actions when hunger reaches a certain point.

Our final "F" is the word that we are just too polite to utter. It is the most famous "F" in the English language; but, for our purposes, will be referred to as **Concupiscence**. This drive like all the other "F" words also erodes conscious control. This impulse is so strong that many silly euphemisms have been erected in its honor -- oops. Often we have heard that the sex act happened "by accident" as if a man with an erection tripped and fell on a naked woman, or my favorite: "Well, one thing leads to another." There is no one thing that leads anything or anyone anywhere – except, of course, the lizard brain.

At the same time, note that the urge to reproduce is an important drive for all species. Until very recently in human history, attrition has been so high for all populations that, without constant replacement, there would be many fewer species than there are today. In fact, geologists point to an unknown event tens of thousands of years ago that wiped out most of humanity. They conjecture that our current population has evolved from only a relative handful of surviving mating pairs who eventually led to a second migration out of Africa. We are all, very literally, made from the same stuff. Evidence that every reptilian impulse has a salutary reason for its existence and concupiscence is no exception. Let's not knock sex.

The Amygdala is the important structure in the Reptilian brain that directs all these "F" responses. In a sense, it is the command center of the reptilian brain. It acts as a sort of clearing house for the realm of the Five "Fs." Once excited with electrical impulses and blood, the Amygdala can command the whole brain. And nowhere does this structure have more power and influence than in the not-yet-fully-formed adolescent brain.

Beginning around age 14, the amygdales – actually, there are two, one in each hemisphere and both about the size of an almond - start to grow rapidly in both boys and girls. For the next four or five years, it has a great impact on both sexes which, in an evolutionary sense, is entirely appropriate. For most of human history, life was both brutal and short; and the survival of the race depended on early breeding. Times have changed, of course. Nowadays, early sexual experiences almost invariably interfere with the extra schooling and training an individual needs to be successful in today's complex society. Just because the individual is physically ready for sex doesn't mean they are emotionally or intellectually ready to take on the challenges that come with it.

We all know what good sense dictates, but the Reptilian Brain is a powerful force to resist; and it is just one of the powerful tides washing over teenagers. During these years, a teen experiences radical transformations -- physically, cognitively and emotionally. Boys often become more physically aggressive. This harkens back to those ages when they would be just entering "training" to assume their roles as hunters and warriors. But in a today's society, these exhibits are a bit like putting a bucket on one's head and running into a brick wall -- which, of course, teenage boys have been known to do at the urging of their peers. You can get a very clear and dramatic sense of what the Amygdala does to boy behavior just by looking at "Jackass the Movie" or any short "Jackass" video on YouTube.

One day before my Shakespeare class, I asked two student aides to help me with a little Amygdala experiment. I asked them to take two plastic prop swords and to stand on either side of the entrance to class. I told them to ask each student who entered to allow themselves to be hit on the head with the flat of the swords. I enjoined that they could not actually hit them but only to ask. The results: every boy said "yes," and every girl said, "no."

Again, this behavior is not as meaningless and mindless as it may appear. It has sound evolutionary origins. It's at about this age that boys begin to develop their leadership skills and engage in male tribal bonding behaviors that were so necessary in primitive societies.

By contrast, girls become more mercurial, flirtatious, communicative, sensitive and emotionally needy. Mood shifts and powerful emotional displays become more common. Although many girls may not display varied emotional states externally, they often experience deep feelings and mood swings that they keep to themselves. That can be more harmful still because these girls often assume that they are the only ones to have such feelings. They feel embarrassment and wonder what's wrong with them alone, unaware that many of their peers are experiencing exactly the same thing. Sudden, inexplicable tears or angry expressions that seem out of proportion to precipitating events are common for Amygdala-influenced females. Another alarming effect of the Amygdala's influence is increased sexual risk-taking by both boys and girls.

Malcolm in the Middle

Next in the Triune system is the mid-brain, which is called the Mammalian Brain where "tribal" behaviors are learned and expressed -- mostly unconsciously. This part of the brain, when active, is the greatest nuisance to teaching and learning higher order cognitive tasks in both teens and adults. The mammalian part of the brain is intensely socially involved, so you can imagine its impact on 14-year-olds.

It determines the way we walk, how we accent our words, how we gesture, how loud we speak, what clothes we wear and when we wear them along with our sensitivity to a thousand other subtle social signals. In a sense, the mammalian brain is a social sensor. Boys at my first high school could, in a moment's notice, slide into the "pimp limp." It was a way of walking made famous and cool by a noted New York pimp who limped because of an injury sustained by one of his "ladies." Although there was no manual or formal classes conducted to teach this stride, boys of all races became facile in its execution by "mammalian osmosis."

The mammalian brain learns mostly by a non-conscious, non-neo-cortex type of learning. We all sense this as context-appropriate behavior in certain situations and we know it to be inappropriate in others. Most of us sense that slang or vulgar language is appropriate in the locker room, but that another dialect and another form of physical expressiveness is called for in SAKS Fifth Avenue or at church. Many children -- boys, in particular -- discover the diabolic delight of farting or laughing out loud in church because these behaviors break a taboo established by the mammalian code of behavior for that environment.

Mammalian behaviors are central to the establishment of culturally appropriate actions as well. Dancing at a family gathering is relatively rare for many Anglos, but more common in Latin cultures or those of African descent. The movie "My Big Fat Greek Wedding" illustrated the clash of cultural norms that are so deeply imbedded in our identities. Some cultures kiss more than others; some stare at you in bars; some find no discomfort pressed against you in a bus or train.

What is noteworthy about the mammalian brain is that, when it is active, the neo-cortex is off for the most part. Even the reptilian brain, although always alert, is in a passive state. Picture kids chatting before class or adults socializing after work; they are mammalian in focus and activity. Children and teens get very sophisticated in their efforts to appear as if they are in an advanced neo-cortex state doing challenging school work, while actually they are secretly texting, passing notes or using any number of gestures or signals to communicate in the mammalian mode.

Small wonder that this part of the brain is often the most common source of distraction and impediment to learning in class. Appearing cool to one's peers and reinforcing those social bonds seems infinitely more important to the adolescent mind than geometry or grammar. This is why it is important to include a social element in teen learning -- group activities or peer-dependent assignments. You'll find that, the more you engage the mammalian brain, the less you'll have to fight it.

On the plus side, this part of the brain takes much less energy and focus to engage than the neo-cortex. Just recall a time when you were in class working on a difficult task and a boy falling out of his chair or a cell phone ringing interrupted you. Your brain switches from the effort-laden rigor of your neo-cortex and checks out the social environment, making eye contact, waving, talking or maybe laughing. Then recall how much effort it took to get back on the advanced brain's task. Socializing and checking in on other humans is much less taxing than thinking and just plain more fun.

New Kid

Finally, the last of the three parts of the Triune Brain is the aforementioned neo-cortex. Called Neo because it is regarded as the "newest" part of our evolutionary brain, it is the seat of "executive" functions or self-control -- what neuroscientists call "emotional self-regulation" or "affect mitigation." This is also the area most engaged in complex conscious learning. It is also busy solving sophisticated linear as well as multi-faceted personal problems such as advanced math or challenging issues of identity or inter-relational problems. You are using this part of the brain if you are reading dense complex material, writing complex ideas or researching, arguing or problem solving. Basically, the central task of American schooling has been the growth and utilization of this last section of the Triune mind.

A teenager's neo-cortex is in growth mode through much of the adolescent pilgrimage. They are just not done yet, duh! Most importantly, the frontal portion of this neo-cortex, which scientists call the pre-frontal cortex (PFC) or the "executive function" portion of their brain, is simply not done forming. The commander of their "starship" brain is still incubating. Poor, incomplete wiring, and an unfinished "commander" make these poor adolescents victims of nature's timing. Actually, nature seems a bit malevolent in the timing of Amygdala vs. PFC growth. The crazy, emotional amygdala is growing and wreaking havoc while the part of the brain that is meant to control its impulses is not "on-line" yet. The PFC directly controls, mitigates or "socializes" the amygdala impulses. That's why teenagers seem nuts to us.

Johnny's heated desire to touch Tammy's leg is only moderated by his still unfinished PFC and, often, a scolding comment from Tammy or a school employee. Most high schools respond to this amygdala world with rules like: "No excessive affection, fondling or kissing allowed," among many others, like "No running with buckets on the head."

So when is a PFC in a male sufficiently developed so he doesn't need the above affection rule or a teacher to correct him? When I have asked educators this across the country the first answer is 50 or 60 years, which is then followed by laughter. The research states that an average boy's neo-cortex would finish growing around age 26 -- assuming he didn't over-use drugs and alcohol. Most boys and girls will, at least, experiment with alcohol; and many will try marijuana especially now that it seems to be gaining social acceptance.

Both of these substances, when used to excess, can significantly impair the function AND THE GROWTH of the neo-cortex. This retards the delicate balance between the primitive impulses of the reptilian Amygdala and the PFC. Drugs foul up the growth of "Adult" circuitry between and among all three major regions of the brain. But nowhere is more complex circuitry needed than between the PFC and the Amygdala. That gradual observable maturation you have witnessed in yourself and others passing through the twenties is precisely the result of new neural-pathways growing in the frontal area of the cranium. When alcohol or marijuana turns off the neo-cortex, the result is the same as disconnecting a computer power cord during a download of new software. The complex and dynamic maturation of these areas and how they relate to each other simply stops.

If you have any experience with chronic drug or alcohol abusers, you may have noticed that those who struggle with drugs often have "missing pieces" in their social and emotional selves. Many lack maturity in important areas – especially, areas of emotional control or adult social and interpersonal behaviors. People who chronically engage in drug abuse for years often have great difficulty ending their addictions because, when they stop using drugs, they experience emotional turmoil. They start feeling and acting like a teenager again. Because the drugs impairs neo-cortex growth, the abusers behavior and feelings appear less adult and more akin to the attitudes and actions of an adolescent – the same adolescent that they were when they began the substance abuse.

This leads to the Perfect Storm of Adolescent Challenge. First, their brains are suddenly under the growing influence of the wild Amygdala with moments of crazy behavior and feelings they have never experienced before. Often parents will declare, "What happened to my little cute Billy?" Well, Billy is no longer and will no longer be the same. He left on the "reptilian train."

Secondly, teens identities are morphing; and they too wonder at times, "Where did little me go?" They challenge authority more but, ironically, with this increased sense of personal power comes a fear of responsibility. They want to be independent; but, at moments, are scared to death of it. They want very much what they don't want, and they live this contradiction in a very awkward and disorienting ebb and flow.

They also suffer the onslaught of hormones both sexual and social, which urge them to "fit in." They suddenly "MUST HAVE" the right clothes, right electronics etc. What results is a schizophrenic person that demands, "Leave me alone, I'm old enough!" AND "Can I have some money and attention?" Parent and teacher heads spin. But consider, for a moment, the deep nature of this perfect storm. Along with struggling with new impulses, identity, power and authority, the teen also must navigate sexual desire, pimples and the humiliation of not being accepted. Right when the amygdala is sending out strong commands to pursue others romantically, hormones are creating blemishes, pimples, changing voices; they are getting uneven hair growth in strange new places and rapid -- and sometimes, embarrassing -- changes are taking place in the body. This body change ironically runs counter to their urges to look great on a date or to outshine someone else. Mother Nature really has a sense of humor!

All of these challenges occur pretty much at the same time. Truly it is a wonder that young people are not worse off than they appear. Knowing all this also helps us know why drugs and alcohol become so attractive. My gosh, just attempting to be social, by itself, is complex and awkward because the social tools they possessed before the amygdala started its rampage are woefully inadequate for what they face throughout the teen years. Adolescents ache to look "cool" which means appearing strong, relaxed and confident during a period of time when they are none of these.

As Albert Camus perceptively stated they "spend an inordinate amount of effort to appear normal."

Alcohol can make struggling teens, actually anyone, feel socially adept. Under the influence, teens generally are NOT socially adept, but the feeling that they ARE socially successful is what hooks them to drinking. Perhaps, the lingering influence of " happy hour" in our culture is the result that even few adults have successfully mastered the art of being successfully social without alcohol. Perhaps, it's because they have never allowed themselves to grow new neural pathways with the brain in the "ON" – not the "alcoholized" "OFF" position.

Who among us can't recall feeling anxiety, low to high, at a large social function BEFORE we drink? How much more anxious a confused teen must be during a similar social gathering? A neuroscientist who studied alcohol's effect on rats found that social interaction increased among rats that consumed alcohol. He also found that certain rats, around 5-to-7% developed an immediate attachment to alcohol and drank to excess (to the point of unconsciousness) each time they were exposed to it. This percentage of alcohol "lovers" is mirrored in teens, especially boys, who too often lack the socially complex behavior and interpersonal awareness of peer feelings that females do. So teens will use alcohol to feel less anxiety in their already awkward social interactions. In spite of the fact that their behavior probably becomes more inept, the fact is they FEEL better about their situations.

The "Catch 22" for these poor humans is that their neo-cortexes are essentially in the "off" position while they are drunk; so any social learning, any socially comfortable behaviors, are not being learned. Social drinkers lock themselves in for the long haul, and generally need their "edge" to be "taken off" for most social gatherings. More troubling is the fact that a minority of teens may have the genes that make alcohol an intense pleasure and this initial social need may transform into a life of addictive alcoholic dysfunction.

Two important points need to be made regarding the difficult emotions of the adolescent pilgrimage, and drugs and alcohol that subdue this pain. First, adolescent, and adult brains, need to suffer the painful challenges of growing. There's no substitute for experience. Boys' brains need to learn that running into a wall with a bucket on their heads is painful, jarring and possibly bloody. Girls need their brains to experience the varied emotional states in order to build new, adult, emotionally stable neural-circuits. The boy needs new neural-pathways that help him say, "Wow, this bucket-on-the-head thing is really stupid!" The female brain needs to experience these sweeps in mood in order to build new circuits to balance them out emotionally.

In short, we need to experience the variations and difficulties of life or our brains will not mature. Therefore, shutting off the brain during suffering is generally a bad idea. This is also why people with chronic abuse problems have twice the difficulty when they stop their substance abuse. First, they miss the pleasurable habit of the drug, AND they have to face emotions they covered up or avoided with drugs or alcohol in the first place.

This is why our roles as teachers and other educational professionals must be greater than our job descriptions. We absolutely must aim our hearts and souls towards becoming mentors as well. Teachers and other educators need to know that a teen may act ridiculous for months or years because of their PFC and amygdala developmental dance. We need to face the fact that our verbal and structural input into their lives MAY NEVER SHOW ANY POSITIVE EFFECT while we know them.

For many teachers this sense of futility with regard to teen behavior can be emotionally draining, especially with no clear signs that a student is growing or changing. Teachers can become burned-out or cynical. We need to know *all interventions have an effect*. The problem for the educator is that the positive effect we have on students will likely not be realized until the young adult has left us. Remember girls become "human" after age 20 or so, and boys around 26-30 years.

As educational leaders, we have to accept that we must stay in a good-faith battle for adulthood with our charges NO MATTER HOW MUCH IT SEEMS POINTLESS. In as much as positive input, from talk, praise, correction and care are given to the student, there is an effect on their brains -- slow and unsatisfying, perhaps, but it is there. All that we do as a class, a school, a village, has an effect on the eventual success or failure of our young people. What we allow and what we don't allow is directly responsible for their growth or stagnation. We just won't see the positive effects most of the time.

Of course, all this seems focused solely on the growth and well being of the child. Well, what about adults who suffer along with the students? This reward - less effort seems too painful at times. Here is where suffering in the adult can be as transformative for the adult as it is for the student. Every time you struggle with a kid, who may even push all of your "buttons," you grow as well. Yet, you grow the most when you don't give-up.

When you hang on in **good faith** with people who "get to you," there is a prize eventually in your own growth. You become more complex and dynamic because "you have gone there." As Zora Neale Huston says in her book *Their Eyes Were Watching God*, "you have to go there to know there." After experiencing difficult interactions, you gain deep conscious and unconscious insight. Yes, this is accompanied by pain; but, oftentimes, pain is the only way to insight, insight that guides you anew when you meet "dirty" Johnny again in a different child.

Adults keep learning, too from their mistakes and from the difficult challenges they face. Parker Palmer, in his book *The Courage to Teach*, says we have to work "until a larger love arrives." Basically, we as educators have to face that this vocation of guiding and teaching students is often difficult and has moments of great suffering. We have to have the courage to persist, especially when the task is most taxing because our brains are hard at work seeking new ways to deal and succeed in this vocation.

Indeed, while we feel frustrated or even miserable during one of these challenging times at school, the unpleasant feelings, that sense of dread, is the direct result of hormones and other chemicals cascading from our brain which is trying to solve the problem or come to a knew way of understanding. The "yucky" sensation is a byproduct or symptom of our busy brain driving to learn anew. We need to persist at these times - to hang in there because a new solution is in the making. Often, the new awareness or new understanding comes to us in the morning.

"The darkest hour is before the dawn."

This saying is actually supported by brain science, now. They know that sleep is a time when the brain can be active in solving problems – even math problems. A study was conducted recently aimed at finding what function sleep had on complex problem solving. Two groups considered similar in many measures were taught how to do a nine-stage math problem. Once each group was clear in their understanding of how to do the nine stages, one group was sent out for six hours of playing ping-pong or other games. The other group was asked to sleep for as much of those six hours as possible. After the six hours, the "playing games" group returned and 27% of this group had figured out how to do the nine-step problem in four stages. Of the sleep group 68% woke up suddenly aware that the problem could be done in only four steps. The sleep group had somehow enabled their brains to search for a more economic method of solving the math problem *by sleep alone*.

Furthermore, the scans done on sleeping brains have shown great activity occurring in the brain, especially if the task or problem is engaged just before bedtime. Well, our challenges with difficult students AND adults are similar to very complex math problems. If you persist in engaging the challenging person, your brain *will create* a new approach, and the answer will most likely be a solution or method you had never tried before. This is the essence of the creative process. Dealing with people in the complex and multi-faceted reality of classrooms and schools is a deep challenge. Interpersonal relationships, combined with the dynamic of leading and teaching, requires more skills and understanding than any of us posses when we first enter the schoolyard.

The goals and tasks of schooling are varied and complex. From inter-cultural understanding, to discipline, teaching methods, supports (for students and teachers) among many other competing and intertwined academic elements, educating is just plain hard. This task of educating is organic, ceaselessly changing and is often a moving target. Schools are not the same as they were 10, 20, or 50 years ago. Technology, demographics, and history are continuing to change. Educators have no choice but to try out their best dance steps in this new cotillion.

Creative and Linear Problem Solving

Grigori Perelman, a noted and unusual Russian mathematician, recently solved a 100-year-old math problem called the Poncaré Conjecture. Mathematicians had troubled over this geometric puzzle since 1904. In 2005, Grigori was stepping on a bus and suddenly he had a flash awareness that he could prove, without question, Poncaré's conjecture.

Perlman had been troubling over this challenge, among many others, for years. On the day he had his epiphany, he was not consciously thinking about solving the problem, but his preconscious brain was hammering away at it. All of our brains work this way. *And, although the left and right cerebral hemispheres work simultaneously and together nearly all the time*, for the purposes of understanding two forms of problem solving we will call Perelman's solution a right–brained or creative solution. Once the scientific and mathematic communities scrutinized his proof, he was awarded the first Clay Millennium Prize Problems award. In spite of this rare honor, he declined to accept out of humility, stating that many others had chipped away at this problem and indirectly contributed to his solution. All of those people deserved recognition too.

However, his solution, which was a century in the making, had now become a known formula - a left-brain permanent file. His solution moved from the right brain's creative, parallel processor and was ensconced in the linear processing, left brain's file box, entitled "what we know." Basically, the right hemisphere creates answers and the left stores these gems. Again, the two sides work together nearly all the time but, for the sake of easy understanding, we are using these generalizations.

So solving problems with the left-brain goes like this: a puzzle/problem presents itself. The left-brain rustles through its huge database of past experiences looking for a quick solution -- partial or complete. You can see how those with larger stored databases of "what we know" can solve more problems. Those with more stored experiences have more left hemisphere files to search through. A plumber looking at a sewer problem under someone's house can often determine an answer based on his experiences from past struggles. Remember the words "past struggles."

However, when Joe the Plummer is asked how to save data on a brand new computer with a crashed hard drive, his left brain will probably be useless based on his set of experiences. Joe will hit the wall. He will stare dumbfounded and feel the "yucky" feelings of confusion and inadequacy. Conversely, Grigori would also have a problem solving plumbing problems, given his life experiences. What both of them would have to do is begin right-brained processing. They will begin to "trouble" over an answer. They will experience confusion, perhaps frustration and anxiety, and be bothered until a suitable answer is found.

With this way of solution making, Joe or Grigori must ***stay interested*** in finding an answer even though they have none. They could start by perhaps talking with experts, and/or talking with those who have experience in the area or subject be it computer hard drives or plumbing. They also might read up on the topic, or approach it systematically by writing down what they know versus what they don't understand. They may create drawings or symbols of the subject at hand. If they took these multi-pronged approaches, they would eventually figure out how to save data on the crashed computer or fix the pipes. They would also have new files in their "what we know" databases of their left brains.

Right-brained problem solving is often difficult because the process itself generally takes time and because of the aforementioned discomfort associated with not having a ready answer. Shakespeare describes this state of unfinished mental business rather harshly: "The genius and the mortal instruments are then in council; and the state of man, like to a little kingdom, suffers then the nature of an insurrection."

As a mentor teacher and staff developer for Advancement Via Individual Determination or AVID, I have heard too many teachers speak the words, "Oh, I've tried that, it doesn't work." We humans often give up way too easily. We aren't comfortable with the process, which is more creative and process-oriented than we like. Our comfort bias sometimes expects results - tangible, measurable progress — sooner than is reasonable. More to the point, often, so do our bosses.

I recall when I was studying Tang Soo Do Karate, and I was getting impatient with my rate of progress up the belt levels: brown, then red and finally black belt. I voiced my concern with my teacher, Master Jong Lee, a Korean ex-Marine with an 8th degree black belt. I opined that my performance and skills merited black belt candidacy. Jong's response was to grab one of his black belts and throw it at me saying, "You want a black belt? Here is a black belt! Now leave!"

I was in my twenties and wanted everything, now. I wanted the reward, the sign of completion and accomplishment. Master Jong was frustrated with me because he was trying to teach me that the reward was in the struggle for perfection, the personal challenge and personal, rather than public, sense of accomplishment.

We, as a nation are increasingly impatient - what with instant messaging, online communication, commerce and even education, which just gets faster and more efficient by the day. The deeper reason for our collective discomfort is the fact that right brained processing is not only time-consuming, it also leaves us vulnerable for a time, without answers, direction or certainty. The left brain in all of us loves solid ground and knowing what to do, AND sometimes we need to tolerate the momentary internal "insurrection" Shakespeare refers to. Dr. Jill Bolte-Taylor, a noted neural-anatomist who suffered a stroke in her left hemisphere, explains this well in her book *My Stroke of Insight*:

"One of the natural functions of my right mind is to bring me new insight in this moment so I can update old files that contain outdated information…Many of us make judgments with our left hemisphere and then are not willing to step to the right (that is into the consciousness of our right hemisphere) for a file update. For many of us, once we have made a decision, then we are attached to that decision forever. I have found that often the last thing a really dominating left hemisphere wants to do is share its limited cranial space with an open-minded right counterpart!"

Once we accept the occasional reality that we must sometimes trouble over complex problems, the discomfort diminishes. Once we accept that this is how our brains work, we can live more comfortably with the challenging aspects. Indeed, many times, very complex problems can be solved in a much more pleasant way called, "play." When Bach was composing he often referred to the process of writing a very complex piece as playing. Picasso noted that as many other artists trouble over trying to find or create the "ultimate" piece of art, he would just play around with shapes, color and design. Picasso liked his process to create art as rummaging around in a garbage heap, looking for something that stands out to him.

The late and brilliant, Nobel recipient Dr. Richard Feynman was inspired by a random event in a college cafeteria where a student threw a dinner plate in the air. This plate rotated a certain way and this triggered his right brain to search further for a solution to a problem he had been working on:

"I started to play with this rotation, and the rotation led me to a similar problem of the rotation of the spin of an electron according to Dirac's equation, and that just led me back into quantum electrodynamics, which was the problem I had been working on. I kept continuing now to play with it in the relaxed fashion I had originally had done and it was like taking the cork out of the bottle – everything just poured out, and in very short order I worked out the things out for which I won the Nobel prize."

Other greats such as Salvador Dali and Thomas Edison also knew about how to access answers from their right minds. Edison would have a notebook next to his bed so he could write down ideas whenever he awakened at night or in the morning. Dali would lie down on a couch with a metal spoon in his hand and a metal dish placed on the floor below his hand. Whenever he would nod off and the right hemisphere began playing around, the spoon would fall from his grasp and hit the metal dish with a loud clang. This would waken him whereupon he would quickly write whatever he just was "thinking" in his dream state. That is how he got some of those bizarre ideas for his surrealistic paintings.

The Ultimate Non-Linear Task of Teaching: Inspiring and Motivating
Since trying to motivate, inspire and teach is such a complex undertaking, most educators have no choice but to engage in a great deal of right-brained problem solving. In Chapter 3, we will explore a math problem grading challenge which will illustrate the multiple levels of challenge in educating young people and running schools.

There are many fuzzy questions in teaching and in organizing a school. For instance, how much do you sacrifice the group for the individual and vice versa? For those children who are struggling for any number of reasons, how much time do you devote to them and neglect the rest of the class? A new teacher really struggles with this among many other "Catch 22s." Yet, it is precisely through these struggles that the new teacher becomes a master or mentor.

"Struggle" is the key word here. We don't honestly use this word, or the word "suffering" much in describing educational vocations. We need to face the fact that teaching hurts; it can wear you out; it can drown you in cynicism and burn you out, unless you call this vocation what it is, and know that there is hope for more and better solutions to the challenges of educating. Just trust your mind. Maintain your intentions because the brain will work itself to those goals because that is how it is designed. Here are three quotes which speak directly to the reality of right-brained problem solving and enduring those times when answers are not readily at hand:

"It is by going down into the abyss that we recover the treasures of life"

-Joseph Campbell
Expert in Myth and Fables

"Without strength to endure the crisis, one will not see the opportunity within. It is within the process of endurance that opportunity reveals itself."

-Chin-ning-chu
Noted business consultant

There is an old educational saying that goes, the mediocre teacher tells; the good teacher explains; the great teacher demonstrates; the superior teacher inspires.

"Have patience with everything unresolved in your heart and try to love the questions themselves as if they were locked in rooms or books written in a very foreign language. Don't search for the answers, which could not be given to you now, because you would not be able to live them. And the point is to live everything. Live the questions now. Perhaps then, someday far in the future, you will gradually, without even noticing it, live your way into the answer."

-Ranier Maria Rilke
Writer

All three of these great passages speak specifically to how we find the solutions to complex issues and how time and discomfort are inescapable parts of the process. Generally, it takes more time than we readily have patience for. We don't like this patience stuff, but we have little choice. In solving the richest challenges, our brain needs rich time and continued interest in finding answers. Rilke asks us to continue to "Live the questions now." We have to maintain hope and faith and endure.

The danger is that we drop the ball of hope and go cynical. Cynicism at its core is disappointment entombed within giving up. Cynicism is a dead neutral state. When we go cynical, we stop living the question; our brain realizes this and stops looking for deeper solutions. Yes, growth is hard, but it's far superior to cynicism. Sometimes our own fear of failure also stops our right-brained problem solving. We may indeed come up with a solution or two and they don't go as expected. So we fail to hang around for what Campbell calls our "treasures" because the abyss is unpleasant and we fear our solutions won't work.

John Gardener, Secretary of Health and Education under Lyndon Johnson said, "We pay a heavy price for our fear of failure. It is a powerful obstacle to growth. It assures the progressive narrowing of the personality and prevents exploration and experimentation."

I am not a blind romantic. I know there are problems that may have no answer in our lifetimes but believing that a problem is beyond resolution guarantees it will not be solved. The left brain likes drawing boundaries and limitations, and often doing so is right and good AND the right brain sees only connections, possibilities and hope and oftentimes those, too, are right and good.

So we must stay in faith with the challenges we face, forgive ourselves when we do give up on one problem or another, and continuously renew ourselves with hope and hard work. Another key point: how can we demand of our students that they work hard, hang in here and try to learn new things if we are not doing the very same things? Our lack of integrity will be obvious in how we talk versus how we walk, how we motivate by example and interact with others on a multitude of levels.

Remember how Dr. Jill Bolte-Taylor could sense the intentions and attitude of nurses and doctors with her right mind? Well, students can read you, too, pre-consciously perhaps, but they do "see" you. They are paying very close attention – whether they let on or not.

For Further Exploration

Need to Know: The Brain and Learning

Publications:

Brendtro, L. K., Mitchell, M. L., & McCall, H. J. (2009). *Deep brain learning: Pathways to potential with challenging youth.* Albion, MI: Starr Commonwealth.
[This book describes structures for approaches to maximize learning.]

Deporter, B., & Hernacki, M. (1992). *Quantum learning: Unleashing the genius in you.* New York, NY: Dell Publishing.
[This book focuses on brain based learning theory and practices.]

Doidge, N. (2007). *The brain that changes itself: Stories of personal triumph from the frontiers of brain science.* New York, NY: Penguin Group (USA) Inc..
[This book illustrates with several case studies and research how "plastic" or changeable the brain is.]

Gladwell, M. (2005). *Blink: The power of thinking without thinking.* New York, NY: Little, Brown and Company.
[This book explores the science behind "intuition" and decision making.]

MacLean, P.D. (1990). *The triune brain in evolution: Role in paleocerebral functions.* New York, NY: Springer.
[This book explores the function and origin of the Triune Brain.]

Medina, J. (2008). *Brain rules.* Seattle, WA: Pear Press.
[This book gives practical advice about the science of learning.]

Pink, D. (2005). *A whole new mind.* New York, NY: Riverhead Books.
[This book illustrates the need to utilize the whole brain, especially the creative capacities.]

Taylor, J. B. (2008). *My stroke of insight*. New York, NY: Viking Penguin. [This book describes the recovery of the author from her stroke and illustrates the need to integrate right brained processing in all that we do.]

Willis, J. (2006). *Research based strategies to ignite student learning*. Alexandria, VA: Association for Supervision & Curriculum Deve. [This book gives practical methods of teaching in a brain-based way.]

Websites:

Advancement Via Individual Determination. (2010). *AVID- decades of college dreams*. Retrieved from http://www.avid.org [This site has resources and links to best practices and brain-based learning.]

Cold Spring Harbor Laboratory. (2009). *Genes to cognition online*. Retrieved from http://www.g2conline.org/ [This site is dedicated to neuroscience and has teacher-friendly accessible information. It also has a three-dimensional brain imager to illustrate brain anatomy.]

Medina, J. (2011). *Brain rules: Brain development for parents, teachers, and business leaders*. Pear Press. Retrieved from http://www.brainrules.net/ [This is Dr. Medina's website with videos and interactive information on maximizing brain power.]

Quantum Learning Network. (2011). *What is quantum learning?*. Retrieved from http://www.qln.com/what_is_quantum_learning.html [This site has resources and information on "Quality Learning" which focuses on optimum learning theory and strategies for the whole person.]

Scientific American. (2011). *Scientific American mind.* Retrieved from http://www.nature.com/scientificamericanmind/index.html
[This is the website for a Scientific American publication called "Mind" which features up-to- date neuroscience for the layman.]

Weber, E. (2010). *Brain leaders and learners.* Brain Leaders and Learners. Retrieved from http://www.brainleadersandlearners.com/
[This site contains brain science related to learning and memory]

3

Need to Know: Race and Culture

"We Americans have the chance to become someday a nation in which all radical stocks and classes can exist in their own selfhoods, but meet on a basis of respect and equality and live together, socially, economically, and politically. We can become a dynamic equilibrium, a harmony of many different elements, in which the whole will be greater than all its parts and greater than any society the world has seen before. It can still happen."

Shirley Chisholm
1924-, American Social activist

It's extremely important to understand the skewed demographics of America's teaching corps and the changing classroom dynamics. This chapter is also extremely important given the skewed demographics of America's teaching core. An e-mail I received from an administrator for whom I was conducting staff training noted, "Our student population is quite diverse with the majority being Latinos, about a third Anglos and the rest equal measures of American Indian, Asian (mostly Hmong) and African Americans." But sadly, he added, "our teachers are mostly white females." Nationally, 75% of all teachers are female -- mainly white and only fluent in English.

Not that there is anything wrong with that, as a famous *Seinfeld* episode noted. We have nothing against white females; however, this skewed teaching core is a problem, both for the women teachers and the various cultures represented in her classes. Cultures and their thought patterns and perceptions are sufficiently different to cause a great deal of confusion and misunderstanding. Understanding how "other" cultures *tend* to think, feel and perceive will do much to guide understanding, and reduce intercultural discord in the classroom. Even when we have inspired enough people of all ethnicities to become teachers, so the teaching core reflects what America looks like, culturally, we will need to work at this understanding even more.

In a larger sense, truly, all humans *are* the same: we all breathe, eat, sleep, love, wish to be loved, can be hurt and can get angry. "If you prick us do we not bleed; if you poison us do we not die," as the Merchant of Venice so aptly put it. The challenge is that we are ALSO different. Culture does inform perception, thought patterns and our understanding of the world.

We educators need to teach and aim our lessons at helping people of other cultures understand; master our linear approach which is reflected in k-college level educational materials as well as our culture at large and help them navigate the linear ladder of America. We also must do this without eradicating their native cultures' perception patterns. We need our students to engage and understand thought patterns which will bring success in America AND allow them to see the world in bi-cultural or multi-cultural ways.

So, we are different and we share a common humanity. So what we have here is a "both/and" description of reality, NOT an "either/or" depiction of reality. Nelson Mandela noted in a recent interview that we Americans too often see the world as either black or white. In the case of culture, both realities are true: we are of *different* cultures and we *share* a common humanity. We are different and the same, and understanding how we are different in a non-judgmental way is the key to intellectually and emotionally navigating through a multicultural future in America.

Now, this statement can be taken many ways, ESPECIALLY because it elicits much emotion as well as various rational insights. For clarity's sake, a truth bears stating: that people of different cultures ARE actually different in many important ways; Mexican Americans are different from Anglo Americans; Native Americans are different from both as are African Americans -- and so on and so forth. But it's a necessary fact to recognize.

"He's just not one of us!"
-Excerpt from a blog referring to then candidate Barack Obama during the election of '08

"All God's children, Jew, gentile, protestant, catholic, black, white"
-Dr. Martin Luther King Jr.

Robert Kaplan, Professor Emeritus of Applied Linguistics at the University of Southern California is known for utilizing Applied Linguistics which concerns bridging theory and practice that affects our understanding of the relationship between language form and language use. Over the last several decades during which Applied Linguistics came of age, Kaplan's name has been most widely linked with the concept of 'contrastive rhetoric,' which is the study of variations in written discourse across cultures.

Chief among his insights are his self-described "doodles" or Discourse Patterns, which illustrate culturally specific thought pattern tendencies. His research resulted in some remarkably simple images that depict patterns of thought which different cultures tend to follow. He too hadn't the resources to study all cultures, so he chose a few common ones from around the globe. The ones he detailed were Romance, Asian, Russian, Arab/Semitic, American and British. Here are the "doodles" Kaplan created to illustrate the patterns by which these cultural groups tend to communicate and think:

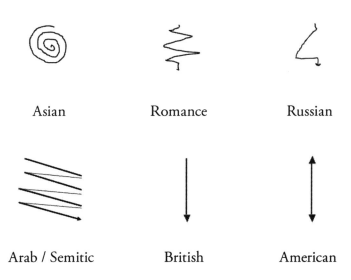

Knowing about these culturally specific patterns has many uses and positive effects. In a significant way, they help reduce culturally myopic feelings of superiority and/or inferiority. They also help us understand the origins of some culturally informed behavior patterns. They inspire us go beyond the attitude that, "*those people* are weird." In addition, they help curriculum designers fashion more successful lessons and interventions for culturally diverse classrooms.

These are clearly NOT all cultural-linguistic groups, nor are they intrinsically better or more important than any other. These simply happen to be the ones Kaplan focused on. What Kaplan does offer through them is part of the answer to this "both/and" challenge that we "are" and "are not" the same human beings that often have varying cultural identities. As you read further, be conscious of judgments that may creep into your thoughts about whether one pattern of thinking is more efficient or superior or even weaker than another, especially your own.

"Asians Talk In Circles!"

Looking at the Asian pattern, mirroring a pinwheel spiral, we see a pattern of thinking and communicating which has as one of its most important elements that of contextualizing. If you consider the pinwheel as the structure of an academic essay or a speech, the main point or thesis occurs at the end where the arrow point is located. Unlike the structure of our academic essays, speeches, sermons, etc, there is no direct statement of the topic or thesis at the beginning of the discourse pattern. The thesis or main idea comes at the end.

Asian

To help in understanding the Asian Discourse Pattern, consider as an example a topic for this pattern: "the usefulness of technology in the classroom." Notice that the topic of technology and its usefulness is mentioned ONLY AT THE END.

In our example, the discourse would begin with a description of the Universe and talk about how, "galaxies fill the cosmos and how these galaxies are super-orbiting systems with billions of stars that circle around in huge discs or spirals and that these orbiting systems are very large in number and that there are galaxies very similar to our own solar system to the degree that their orbs also orbit a center. Only our solar system has but one star at its center with several planets orbiting it; and that, of all the planets orbiting our sun, only one planet has life, and that is our earth; and that the life on earth has evolved a consciousness and that mankind is the most intelligent of the life on earth; and that we humans form societies and cultures; and, in order to educate and pass on the wisdom of man, we create schools; and in these schools various tools and materials are used to educate; and among those tools is the very powerful set of technologies such as computers and the Internet."

Granted, this example is an extreme model of the Asian pattern. However, it accurately describes the Asian approach which contrast so much with our American pattern. This Asian Discourse Pattern example sounds strange to western ears, as much of the information seems off the topic of the "power of technology in the classroom." Didn't you feel yourself wanting to say, "Get to the point, already!" All this talk about the cosmos and planets does not - to us - sound germane or supportive of the point or thesis. The key here is that this pattern of thought is being "descriptive" and not "proscriptive."

What Kaplan and other linguists have discovered is that this pattern "contextualizes" the main topic. This way of organizing information places the topic into a larger context. In our example, computers are literally placed into the larger scheme of things. The primary characteristic of this way of thinking is that it places the topic of "technology" within the context of society, the world, and the universe.

We Western Europeans and Americans are heirs to the Greek's way of compartmentalizing and reducing reality. Science itself is considered "reductive" in philosophy. We reduce complex reality to manageable bits - just as we do when we present information in business meetings and often in schools. We use bullet charts that reduce and separate information into hierarchies of importance removing what we consider irrelevant or unrelated. We often select our targeted ideas or points and information from their larger contexts.

Sir Ken Robinson is an author, speaker and international advisor on education. In 2003, he was knighted for his achievements in creativity, education and the arts. He is a popular speaker at the well- known think tank, TED (Technology, Entertainment and Design) conferences in California. TED's mission statement begins,

"We believe passionately in the power of ideas to change attitudes, lives, and ultimately the world. So we're building here a clearinghouse that offers free knowledge and inspiration from the world's most inspired thinkers and also a community of curious souls to engage with ideas and each other."

At one of Sir Robinson's recent lectures, he showed a photograph of a tiger during his lecture. He only showed it for ten seconds or so. Then he asked us what we saw. All 150 American educated listeners responded that we'd seen a tiger. Sir Ken went on to say that 90% of Western Europeans and Americans report that they had seen a tiger - just a tiger - even though the actual photo also shows a jungle of multicolored trees and bushes. He went on to state that Asians report seeing "a jungle with a tiger in it" or "a tiger in the jungle." This difference is profound in that you realize each culture will perceive reality via their own unique "movie theaters." Again, this is not implying that Anglo Europeans are blind, but it does underline the fact that our two cultures come to conclusions and interpret the world in vary different ways.

This Asian "doodle" of Kaplan's has also happened to make me a bit of a marriage counselor. I was training teachers in Washington State where there is a sizeable population of Asian descendant teachers. Normally, I train mostly Anglo, Latino and African-American teachers. This particular session had only Asians except for one Latino male teacher. Thus, when it came time to teach the Asian pattern, I began to experience a bit of paranoia, thinking that some of the Asian teachers would find my explanation of Asian pattern racist or biased at the very least.

After explaining the discourse patterns before lunch break, three Asian women approached me as the rest of the participants were leaving the class. I got a cold feeling in my gut fearing that I had indeed appeared racist or was stereotyping. I sat down awaiting a harsh verdict when one of the three spoke up and said, "Mr. Madigan, we are all from Taiwan, and we all happen to have married Anglo men. You have just described a problem we have been having with our husbands. Whenever they ask us questions, we feel we have to give the "whole" answer. And he only wants a short piece of the answer!"

I was so relieved and amazed! A more personal, real and exact validation of Robert Kaplan's work, I have never heard. One wonders how many misunderstandings, feelings of isolation, and self-doubt or recrimination occurs within Asian children as they navigate American schools and society. These three grown women felt liberated and had new insight into their husbands after my short description of Kaplan's powerful insight. They went on to say that their Anglo men wanted short concise answers without the context. Their men wanted "bullet" answers. One of the three women was actually in tears describing how she and her husband had even discussed divorce because of this recurring problem.

Keep in mind that all three women spoke perfect English. Their challenge was NOT the language but the pattern biases that each culture had. In addition, what is interesting is how many of the most important religious and political symbols of the Asian world are circular in nature like the discourse pattern: the yin-yang symbol, Buddha's Eight-fold-path wheel, the Japanese flag, the Korean flag and others. The obvious challenge for we educators is to erect a scaffold to support Asian students and adults though the use of graphic organizers and other visuals as they accommodate to the American pattern. Being aware of these thought pattern tendencies helps students and teachers of "other" cultures identify and navigate moments of intercultural discord as well as harmony between the two ways of perceiving information.

"Mexicans Tell lots of Stories!"

Victor Villasenor, author of *Rain of Gold*, among many other novels and memoirs, loves to tell stories. I remember the first time I saw one of his talks: I was mesmerized by his engaging tales of his grandmothers, his father, his dog, his horse, his teachers, and on and on. The stories themselves did not SEEM like they were going anywhere; but they were filled with passion and, suddenly he would declare, "that's how I know you all are geniuses!" or "that's how I know there is the possibility of world peace for 5,000 years!"

At those moments when he ends his speech with a passionate declaration, you would suddenly sense, "Oh, I get it! That's what that story meant!" Somehow, something that you were not conscious of in your head suddenly coalesced in your psyche and it occurred to you, "Wow, he's right!" Victor is a prime example of the Romance or Latin Discourse Pattern. The message arrives like a lightening bolt. You are lulled by story after story, anecdote after anecdote, metaphor after simile, image after symbol, with long visually stunning and flowery style until, like a bolt of lightning you get it. Bang! The thesis at the end -- not unlike like the Asian's roundabout approach. Like the Asian pattern, the Latin pattern also seems to wander off-topic to North Americans, straying too far away to be cohesive.

Romance

Another great example is the first few pages of *One Hundred Years of Solitude* by Gabriel Garcia Marquez. His sentences seem unending and to meander. What's fascinating is that these first pages contain the description of a river - winding, swirling and meandering, just like the Latin discourse pattern itself. I have encountered this pattern often over the years as a teacher reading the essays of my Latino students. I remember one great example in which a college application required a student to write about a person they admire – note: "a person." Marco, who was one of the best writers I had ever taught, wrote about his grandfather, grandmother and his little sister; and read his essay aloud to the class. Somehow, it worked, even though he strayed a bit from the commission; and his reading of it received kudos from his fellow students. Even though he was specifically told to focus on a single person, his effort was so sweet, authentic and created for us such a powerful set of personalities that I recommended he send it unaltered.

I remember asking him why he didn't focus on one of the three family members, and he told me, "They [grandma/grandpa/sister] are all connected. I don't know how I could separate them." Somehow, he had been able to describe all three family members in such a way that they magically commingled as one.

Both of the two schools that accepted him took the unprecedented step of writing to commend him on his remarkable essay. Again, that is a rare occurrence. In my many years of teaching seniors, I know of but a few whose application essays were commented upon by admissions officers. Marco is in his last stages of residency and nearly a doctor, and his Latin discourse pattern did not harm, nor did learning the American way.

Dr. Maria Montano-Harmon of Cal State Fullerton discovered that, even students two and three generations removed from their native homeland, still displayed this Latin pattern. Her dissertation which was based on a linguistic analysis of more than 900 essays written by English-dominant Latinos showed that, even after several generations, this tendency toward meandering stories persisted. As with the Asian thought pattern, students who have the Romance/Latin pattern can be assisted in learning the American pattern by using graphic organizers.

Keep in mind that no pattern is the "right" one. All patterns have the power to communicate and have more or less utility in different social circumstances. Being right isn't as important as being good, much like my student Marco. That said, since the American Pattern is so prevalent in North America, it behooves all students to become proficient in it -- ideally, without losing their ability at self-expression in their native patterns.

As Dr. Montano-Harmon would often state, we educators need to be non-judgmental about these patterns. We need to avoid the impulse to suppress a student's native language or discourse pattern in the effort to teach them a new one. Too many emotional/cultural problems arise within children and adults if their culture is in ANY way demeaned.

Besides, there are benefits to be realized for students able to communicate in the American Pattern in business and certain social situations, while maintaining as much of their native speech patterns as well: to be "bi-discoursal." It's a bit like being ambidextrous or a switch-hitter in baseball. It's an advantage to have both sides of the mind and body balanced since so few of us do. Some research has actually shown that people who are bi or tri-lingual tend to have lower reported incidences of mental illness. Perhaps this is because they have more linguistic/cognitive options or tools to solve life's conundrums.

Certainly thinking in "either/or" or "black/white" ways diminishes your capacity to solve complex, nuanced problems. Those who are proficient in more than one language will recognize that there are many words, concepts, modes of expression, colloquialisms that are not literally translatable -- that each language has its own unique way of thinking and a vocabulary to match. When you speak English, you think in English; and when you speak Spanish, you think in Spanish. And both have something to contribute that the other can't. The two are greater than the sum of their parts. Being proficient in both opens your options.

The Russian nudged you and said, "Do you know what I mean?"
Next, we have the Russian mode of thinking and communicating. A great way of exemplifying the Russian Pattern is to refer to the famous George Orwell story *Animal Farm*. Although this tale is not Russian, it's a great example of the pattern. Ostensibly, it is a story about actual farm animals on a farm. But, of course, they are not animals. The barnyard's inhabitants are anthropomorphized and adopt all the worst human stereotypes along with a facility for English. No sooner is the farmer gone than the animals form up into two warring camps. One is headed by a few autocratic thugs who lead through force and coercion. The other group is an alliance of like-minded creatures trying to prevent the thugs from taking control of the world, rather, the barnyard. Okay, it's a rather thinly veiled allegory of the period leading up to World War II. Orwell doesn't try very hard to disguise his obvious distaste for the Fascist pigs in the morality play and his approval of the hard-

pressed allies. Hint. Hint. It helps to know that the book was published on the eve of the end of World War II. It is Orwell's clever re-packaging of a familiar historical event, stated indirectly or symbolically.

Russian

The Russian pattern follows this same path, which may explain Russia's rich literary heritage. The Russian pattern displays a rather long and digressive story line which seems to take as long as *War and Peace* to get to the point. Instead of directly stating the core message in clear and unambiguous language, a symbolic or metaphoric representation is unwound and unwound and unwound. It's often a long journey but, at the end of it, we often see what we already know in a new way.

This method of communication also facilitates the discussion of taboo subjects because the taboo is hidden beneath layers of allegory or, as British Prime Minister Winston Churchill once famously noted, "a riddle, wrapped inside a mystery, inside an enigma." It is believed that the style developed from centuries of dictatorial rule in both Czarist and Soviet Russia frank or transparent discussion of many topics -- but must notably politics -- was strictly forbidden. Considering the real threats of death or prison, this indirect form of thought and communication is understandable. Several great writers and poets resulted from this prohibitive environment given the need for symbols and metaphors. A modern example is Andrei Codrescu, author of *The Posthuman Dada Guide* among many other essays and poems, is now an expatriate living writing and speaking in America. Look up some of his work as a living example of this rich way of thinking and speaking.

Cain and Abel spoke the same language – The Arab/Semitic Pattern

Interestingly, Iranian president Ahmadinejad wrote a letter to George Bush a few years ago, and his Secretary of State, Condoleezza Rice, read it. Because this letter's message was a big deal, the story was all over television news. When she spoke, she said something like "I have read President Ahmadinejad's letter and it is a rambling piece." She did not seem to understand anything about discourse patterns, nor had she probably ever hear Dr. Maria Montano-Harmon's request to see other cultures tendencies "non-judgmentally." She was definitely "proscriptive" and critical of the Iranian leader's method and pattern of communicating. Indeed, in the executive summary of "The Consortium for Strategic Communication" at Arizona State University, it states, "The letter was dismissed by U.S. spokespersons as a "rambling" narrative or as a "meandering screed" that did not address the current U.S. concerns over the nuclear energy program initiated by President Ahmadinejad." American diplomats seem ironically ignorant of cultural differences.

Granted, the Iranians are not considered Arabic or Semitic; however, they do share characteristics with the Arab/Semitic pattern. It also merits mentioning that the historical conflicts between the Arabic and Semitic peoples may have some hope for their possible reconciliation simply because they think and communicate with the same pattern.

Arab/Semitic

What identifies this pattern is the continual use of comparisons and contrast, through the structures of similes and analogies: "this is like this which is like this which is different from that which also is like that...

therefore this is true." Like the Asian, Romance and Russian pattern, the thesis occurs at the end, after the comparison contrast "argument" is made. This pattern also utilizes stories of precedent and is also imagistic full of colorful and poetic visuals. You can recognize this pattern in the Bible, especially where Jesus uses parables: "like the birds of the field..." or "this is like the good Samaritan..." Stories and parables are "like" the point being expressed. To our ears this pattern seems to ramble on and on utilizing what seems, to our minds, off topic and filled with superfluous information. What we fail to see with quick dismissive judgments like this is the intricate and complex presentation of information. The primal genesis of this pattern may have its origins in one way that all our brains process new information. We create new understanding by connecting the new learning with the old. We bridge prior knowledge with new information to understand.

This pattern is more complex in structure (as are most of the other patterns) when compared to the American or British paradigms. Again, this is not to say that the British or American patterns are weaker. Rather, they are different and have their own nature of depth and richness.

"Get to the point" and the "straight talk" of the British and American Patterns

As Samuel Clemens, better known as Mark Twain, so poignantly noted: "Britain and America are two countries separated by a common language." Brits and Yanks will immediately recognize the truth of that observation. To their ears, the other seems to be speaking a foreign language. Although this is basically true, Americans and Brits do share very similar discourse patterns. We both present information reductively and linearly. We extract specific facts or inferences that support a position and lay that information out in a straight, linear progression.

The British, however, share a trait common to all the other patterns: the topic focus or thesis is at the end of the piece. The challenge and complexity of this pattern is in the creation of the facts and support used in the pattern. Most of the other patterns utilize stories, illustrations, metaphors and symbolic representations to make their points. The British will reduce or extract just the kernel of information needed to make the point. Instead of allowing stories or narratives to illustrate positions, the British highlight only that which is needed to efficiently make a point. Like a bullet chart of facts and hints leading to a financial statement or conclusion, the British pattern is more succinct and economic in word use. Notice also their frequently clipped speech patterns.

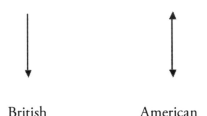

British   American

The Americans also share this linear structure and the tendency to "reduce" a passage only to information germane to the main point. What contrasts the American from the British is this more direct approach of communication. The British may more frequently utilize inference and nuance than Americans. A great example of this American style comes from when Joe Biden reported hearing then-President George Bush, say, "Joe, I don't do nuance." Indeed, Linguists call our style of communicating, "Direct and Confrontative." Unlike the British, we begin with our thesis and end with a restating of our thesis. Our academic essays follow this general pattern:

> ***Tell them what you are going tell them***
> ***Tell them***
> ***Then, tell them what you told them***

This structure is simple -- again, the complex element is the work done in advance in the reductive mind of the writer, speaker or thinker. They need to mine the gem of thought from a sea of information. They have to pull the "bullet" out of the body of information, to find specific supporting facts and evidence that explicitly support their argument or position. Also, in contrast to the British, there are no hints to speak of. This "Direct and Confrontative" style may be why Americans are often perceived as rude or brusque. We get to the point – just like the comedian, *Larry the Cable Guy* says: we "get 'er' done." We are not rude people. We are just very economic and direct. This simple pattern is the pattern/structure expected in all essay assessments both on the high school and collegiate level.

Ironically, in Advanced Placement English and in more advanced college writing courses some elements of the British tendency to imply rather that directly state is valued. In addition, the illustrative qualities common to other cultures is also valued in more advanced writing courses especially with regards to figurative language and use or metaphor. Perhaps, that is why my student Marco had such a warm reception at the college level.

A great story illustrating the difference between the American and British ways occurred when Dr. Harmon, husband of Dr. Maria Montano-Harmon, came from England to teach in a California university. To do so he had to take and pass the "C-BEST" exam administered by the state of California. This exam is intended to check for Basic Educational Skills and must be passed prior to being allowed to teach in any publicly funded school kindergarten through college. Among a myriad of basic skills this exam also assesses essay-writing skills.

Well, Dr. Harmon whose Ph. D. is in English failed the essay portion of the test. As you might imagine, this was a challenging and disorienting fact to accept for Mr. Harmon; however, with the brilliant metacognitive counseling of his wife - an expert in Kaplan's language patterns, she helped him understand that he indeed did not include a thesis at the beginning of the essay. He had written his essay in the British pattern. He knew that he had placed his thesis only at the end of the essay. He had a clear memory of what he had written. When he re-took the test with the new knowledge that there must be two theses framing both the beginning and end of the composition, he easily passed. This event is not only novel and illustrative of the specific and vital differences between two Discourse Pattern' cousins, it also sheds more light on the occasional inefficiency of standardized tests in determining a person's capacities or skills. Again, knowing that these culturally specific ways of thinking and communicating are in our classrooms will help us value various ways of perceiving. Most importantly, knowing about these Discourse Patterns will aid us educators in teaching students of various cultures about the use and understanding of our American Discourse Pattern. Gaining literacy in our pattern will give them greater access to the American dream.

However, the most important benefit is realized when a student learns about these Discourse Patterns because their understanding of their own difficulties suddenly clarifies, just as knowing about these patterns helped the three Taiwanese women in my training sessions in Seattle, Washington.

Gaining this metacognition about why they may be struggling due to culturally different thought patterns de-personalizes their struggle. Realizing that the issue is not their fault, or that nothing is wrong with them is a great relief. Also, knowing the differences between their own pattern and the American pattern gives them more hope and increases the efficacy of learning the American pattern. Thus, it is vital that not only teachers be made aware of Kaplan's Patterns, but students, too.

Generally, when teachers first hear of these patterns they are amazed. The reaction by all educational leaders is the lifting of a great weight -- that an area of great tension and confusion common to our multi-cultured pluralistic society suddenly makes sense.

Intercultural Friction and Racism
Between the days of October sixteen and eighteen in 1991 Croatian civilians slaughtered 24 Serbian civilians in the Croatian town of Gospic.

They killed the fifteen men and nine women with guns, knives and sledgehammers. Afterward they lay the bodies out in rows in the shallow snow, doused them with petrol and set them on fire.

By Goran Mikic with Permission

The Croats were primarily Catholic Christians while the Serbs were Russian Orthodox Christians. Both groups profess to follow the teachings of Jesus of Nazareth who is often referred to as the "Prince of Peace." The Serbs and Croats shared a similar geography and religion and are likely descended from south Slavic tribes. Therefore, they appear fairly similar.

Paying special attention to the words, "knives, sledgehammers" and "set them on fire" the emotions of rage and hate come to mind. There has been a deep and passionate anger or resentment between many who belong to these two "tribes." This bitterness even affects many of these two groups' respective historians who bicker about how *different* they are in origin. Some Croat historians have actually declared that the Virgin Mary gives special recognition to Croats because of a purported visitation/apparition by her to

Croatian children in 1981. This visitation occurred in Medjugoje, in Bosnia Herzegovina which is populated by both ethnic groups as well as Bosnians.

Balkan expert David MacDonald, in his book *Balkan Holocausts: Serbian and Croatian victim-centered propaganda and the war in Yugoslavia*, states "Medjugorje performed several crucial functions in Croatian nationalism. Firstly, it elevated Croatian Catholicism to a chosen and superior religion, and Croatians themselves to the rank of a superior nation." Some Serbs as well have used ancient religious sites to justify savagery such as their Saint Lazar called the martyr of Kosovo who fought and was martyred by the Turks in the 1300s. This saint was one of the justifications for Serbian ethnic cleansing of Albanians living in Kosovo which also led to U.S. military involvement.

The big question is how at risk are we as a pluralistic, multi-ethnic nation to this same animal savagery? In addition, consider how much more potential danger is added to our American national experiment when you look at how different we visually appear to each other as different cultural groups. The Serbs and Croats look similar, and share more attributes than many of the ethnic identities that make up the family of America. What has and does fuel much of the pent-up rage and animosity between these similar groups is not only their versions of Christianity, but their history as well.

Remember how the chapter on cognitive science discussed the amygdala and how fear affects our cognition and behavior? Two important facts bear restating: One, we remember the negative and the threatening far more vividly than anything else. Two, when we are threatened or afraid, our capacity to think in a measured and rational way is severely diminished or shut off completely. Add these two realities: cultural groups that have been attacked or ravaged by atrocities in times of war remember these atrocities just as a single human would. Horrible memories are passed down generation to generation by the retelling of family stories and the anger, and fears are passed with them. Throw in catastrophic societal change or economic stresses that reach a "tipping point" and you have a human time bomb.

Once the Soviet "Bear" left Yugoslavia, ethnic hatred and friction exploded into a 10-year war which may have only been ended by U.S. force. The "peace" we see there now depends much on the threat of NATO force and the U.S. military. As William Blake declares in his poem, *The Human Abstract*, "Mutual fear brings Peace." In the case of the Balkan ethnic groups, embers of retribution may still burn.

For us Americans, our multicultural family does have some painful historical moments. For indigenous Americans, there is a wide held memory of conquest, death at the hands of Europeans as well as the full extinction of certain tribal groups. African Americans know about hundreds of years of forced, unpaid labor and slavery. They too suffered death, and family disintegration under the business model of slave labor. Mexicans know well the history of loss of great swaths of land extending roughly from San Francisco diagonally down to Texas, land many Latinos refer to as "Atzlan." See below the Absolute Vodka ad that enraged many in the U.S.

They also remember prior to the Mexican-American War the war with the French under Emperor Maximilian, and before that with the conquest of their ancestors the Aztecs and Mayans by the Spanish. Octavio Paz, the famous Mexican philosopher says that these conquests have left a wound similar to that of a rape victim, what he calls the "Hijo de la chingada," or son of one raped. Perhaps less like the Croat – Serb conflicts, our inter-ethnic friction has less of a religious nature to it, though. Although Christianity sometimes suffers from those who use her as justification as exemplified by burning, we do not have at this time the level of heated religious fervor that has been present in the Balkans.

What we must remember and face is that once we reach a tipping point where great ethnic strife consumes us and our brains go primal, the behavior of an unchecked amygdala is what you see in those murdered and burned corpses of Serbs. There were many worse atrocities during the Balkan wars, too many to mention where guilt can be placed on every group: Serb, Croat, or Bosnian. The gift we still have in spite of our unpleasant intercultural history is that we have not as an American nation suffered the level or frequency of war horror that Europe has witnessed. This is not to deny or diminish the savagery experienced by Native Americans, African Americans or Latinos. It is just that Europe has been at war for most of its history and, sometimes, for up to one hundred years at a time. It has been the center of two world wars fought in rapid succession.

We are better off, and that blessing must be protected. We do not want the cultural memories that continue to embroil Palestinians and Jews, Catholics and Protestants in Ireland, Hutus and Tutsis in Africa, or any number of other seemingly endless conflicts on this globe. Machiavelli warned that a people will forgive you for the death of their father but they will not forgive you for the taking of their land. We need to share this land. More importantly we have to realize we can avoid the dangers of ancient and undying hatreds if we face our own prejudices and fears, consciously.

Without question, this is difficult to do with individuals and even more challenging with groups or societies. Only education can make any headway in this area. Education is our only hope. For a positive example of change or improvement just remember that 4forty years ago most people were resigned to the ever-present smell of cigarette smoke in airplanes, cars, restaurants. Cigarettes are gone from most public locations. Today smokers are challenged to find ANY legal place to smoke. Indeed, this end to public smoking even occurred in Paris, the home of smoking and eating. If you asked a Parisian fifteen years ago if cafes in Paris would ever be smoke free, he would laugh in your face, yet, in 2008 this unthinkable reality became law. Even more amazing is that the Parisians followed this rule to the surprise of many. Courtney Traub, a Paris travel guide, wrote in her blog in 2008 that, "Most Parisians, though, have adjusted to the change with an ease that has taken everyone by surprise, especially considering the longstanding cultural tradition here of protesting and flouting the rules when possible."

This only goes to show that longstanding and tightly held traditions are not immutable. For an example of open-mindedness and change in the arena of race and ethnicity, look no further than the election of Barack Hussein Obama to the Presidency of the United States. Several of my African-American students openly declared before the election that, "there is no way this country is ready for a black man." Several white and Latino students and teachers as well, confessed the same cynical view. Regardless of your opinion of him as a president, the fact that he won is quite striking considering America's history. In spite of these remarkable alterations to the status quo, taking on racism and cultural friction is still difficult. But again we must aim our nation away from the seemingly endless hatreds that dot this planet by thinking and engaging other ethic groups in positive ways. We also need to look at our own cultural groups anew.

With the hopes of finding answers to our racial ills, a great deal of research has been done on the brain to understand the anatomy of racism -- what causes it and maintains it. Much study has been devoted to understanding "racist affect' or the feelings that we experience when we encounter persons of different cultural groups whether we think we are prejudiced or not. When Obama won the nomination, articles were written about how people of non-black races reacted to his image. Most non-black people hooked up to an fMRI (Functional Magnetic Resonance Imaging ñ which can "see" into the brain and record what areas are active) showed increased Amygdala activity. This reaction is generally accepted as a deep and pre-conscious reaction of fear or alarm.

We ALL are susceptible to this reaction because we all have a basic "baseline" sense of security which came from our first few weeks and months of life. We became programmed, in a sense to our mother's look, sound, smell, color, all that we experienced through our senses. That "programming" is what we perceive as safe or secure. So, basically, we all have preference; we all are innately prejudiced in favor of our group's look and feel. This does not mean that when we are children and meet someone from another race that we feel fear without cause.

Children are remarkably capable of accepting difference. Actually, they crave it with their natural curiosity. However, this does mean that in times of stress or fear that we will gravitate to people like our mothers. Of course if you are from a mother who was threatening from day one, this model gets skewed, negatively. Alternately, if you grew up in mixed racial home, what feels safe will turn out to be more broad and complex, but for most of us, this is a basic predictable truth. You cannot hide your feelings from an fMRI. So, we start out with a deep preference *for* safety from our group, but we are not actively racist or prejudiced *against* anyone. The danger arises as we age and those around us with whom we live or associate, begin to *teach* racist thoughts and feelings. Racism also grows from experiences and *how* we process them.

Objectification vs. Understanding & *External vs. Internal Racism*
Dr Laura Schlessinger said the "N" word eleven times to a caller on her national radio show recently. She did not understand why she could not say

it, but that black males could. The point is Dr. Laura did not understand. However, being a Jew and member of a group that has suffered hate throughout history, you would wish that she would understand. We are all like Dr. Laura, incomplete in our understanding of our fellow ethnic Americans. However, this is precisely why we as a nation need to face our ignorance before we become a Bosnian nightmare. Words like the "N" word objectify. They turn complex people or things into stick figures, devoid of dynamic characteristics. Racial slurs are labels that limit our understanding.

Our left brains love labels and borders, and we need labels and categories for many human activities. Yet, labels are dangerous in race relations and in the process of understanding others. Labels by their nature cannot capture the full dynamic complexity of a human person. We are NOT things, however satisfying it may be to label someone as if they were -- and, make no mistake, it is satisfying to label. We all find it more emotionally satisfying, especially when we are upset or threatened, to label people, to pigeonhole them. It is easier than trying to understand their complexity.

This is the battle that was fought in the minds of many Americans that voted for Obama: was he "just one of those people" or was he a full, complex human being? The part of the brain that did the calculation is called the PFC or the Pre-Frontal Cortex. This is the part of the brain that warns teenage Johnny that there are consequences to touching Tammy's breasts. It's the same part of the brain that told many millions of white Americans, who were "programmed" after birth to find safety in white faces, this Obama guy was okay to vote for. This is also a part of the brain we can control, unlike the fearful and reactive Amygdala. When we regularly "check" our prejudices, when we consider our opinions carefully, this part of the brain actually becomes more complex and capable of mitigating reactive and racial stereotyping. What happens is the brain becomes a better buffer of primitive reactions and it also becomes more creative in how it responds to signals of fear which can end up in fights or worse, like in Gospic Croatia. So simply thinking about what you wish to believe is powerful. Research also says that if you simply picture in your mind, or visualize positive role models of races that you fear, you can also reduce your reactivity. This breaks down the over-simplified labels that cloud our judgments. In addition, joining a team or group that is multi-racial or multi-ethnic has been shown to reduce Amygdala responses in test cases because the "group think" helps erase fear and mistrust.

Most powerful in decreasing fear is meeting and connecting with people of other races and cultures. I remember a day when I asked my students to share a bit about who they were to the rest of the class, and a black male shared that he was a "skater." He loved skateboards. I remember vividly, three white boys gasping at this news. They later confessed that they never knew "black people skated." Well, a week later as I was driving home past the shopping center, there they all were: three white boys and a black boy, skating together ñ all with calm Amygdales.

Finally, the most dangerous and insidious form of racism is not living in the hearts of members of the Klu Klux Klan; the worst racism resides in the hearts of those who suffer from racism. The internal beliefs that guide behavior within each person regardless of race either guide a person to fulfillment or to self hate and misery. This form of racism is called "implicit racism." Many studies of racism are based on the IAT or "Implicit Association Test" which can reveal our unconscious or implicit prejudices. Malcolm Gladwell in his fascinating book *Blink,* which shares great insights about our perceptions and social selves, notes that, "The giant computer that is our unconscious silently crunches all the data it can from the experiences we've had, the people we've met, the lessons we've learned, the books we've read, the movies we've seen, and so on, and it forms our opinions." He goes on to say that those deep experiential biases are "what is coming out in the IAT."

We all have these biases, based on things such as our memories of our mother's faces in infancy, and then throughout our lives. Professor of Psychology at Harvard University, Mahzarin Banaji says, "You don't choose to make positive associations with the dominant group, but you are required to. All around you, that group is being paired with good things. You open the newspaper and you turn on the television, and you can't escape it." For example, Gladwell notes in his book that of the 50,000 African-Americans who have taken the IAT so far, about half of them have more favorable associations with whites than blacks. Beyond joining teams, and visualizing positive role models and challenging yourself to rethink some of your own beliefs, Gladwell offers another more human suggestion that we commit to equality, and that commitment "requires that you change your life so that you are exposed to [other] minorities on a regular basis and become comfortable with them and familiar with the best in their culture, so that when you want to meet, hire, date, or talk with a member of a minority, you aren't betrayed by your hesitation and discomfort."

For Further exploration

What We Need to Face About Culture and Racism

Publications:

Gay, G. (2010). *Culturally responsive teaching: Theory, research, and practice.* New York, NY: Teachers College Press.
[This book explores the research and practical elements of effective education in the pluralistic classroom.]

Holzman, M. (2010). *Yes we can: The 2010 schott 50 state report on black males in public education.* Schott Foundation for Public Education, (http://blackboysreport.org/).
[This is a report on the state of Black students in America.]

Kaplan, R. (2002). *The oxford handbook of applied linguistics.* New York , NY: Oxford University Press.
[The author clearly demonstrates the varied thought patterns specific to different cultures.]

Kelley, D., Machery, E., & Mallon, R. (2010). *Racial cognition and normative racial theory.* Oxford Handbook of Moral Psychology
[This report evaluates the results of various research into racism.]

Rodriguez, R. (1992). *Days of obligation: An argument with my mexican father.* New York , NY: Penguin Books.
[This book explores the conflicts and challenges of being multi-racial.]

Singleton, G.E. & Linton, C. (2006). *Courageous conversations about race: A field guide for achieving equity in schools.* Thousand Oaks, CA: Corwin Press.
[The book focuses on a conversation that most schools avoid.]

Thomas, P. (2003). *The skin i'm in: A first look at racism*. Hauppauge, NY: Barron's Educational Series, Inc.
[This introduces the multi-cultural world we live in to children.]

Trepagnier, B. (2007). *Silent racism: How well-meaning white people perpetuate the racial divide*. Boulder, CO: Paradigm Publishers.
[This book argues that "heightened race awareness is more important in changing racial inequality."]

Villasenor, Victor (1991). *Rain of gold*. New York , NY: Dell Publishing.
[This is the story of two families migrating north from central Mexico to the southern U.S. during the Mexican Civil War.]

U.S. Department of Education: Institute of education Sciences. (n.d.). *National assessment of educational progress: The nation's report card*. Retrieved from http://nces.ed.gov/nationsreportcard/
[This is a national assessment of educational progress with some emphasis on cultural and ethnic populations.]

Websites:

Advancement Via Individual Determination. (2010). *AVID- Decades of college dreams*. Retrieved from http://www.avid.org
[Their mission is to close the achievement gap by preparing ALL students for college readiness and success in a global society. They have educational trainings for cultural awareness.]

Anti-Defamation League. (2011). *ADL: Fighting anti-semitism, bigotry and extremism*. Retrieved from http://www.adl.org/

Movimiento Estudiantil Chican@ de Aztlán. (2011). *Movimiento estudiantil chican@ de Aztlán*. Retrieved from http://www.nationalmecha.org/
[This is a student support organization for Latinos.]

Southern Poverty Law Center. (2011). *Southern poverty law center.* Retrieved from http://www.splcenter.org/
[Information and resources on race and ethnicity in America.]

4

Radical Balance: Standardization AND Personalization

"The illiterate of the 21ˢᵗ century will not be those who cannot read and write but those who cannot learn, unlearn and relearn."
-Alvin Toffler, author of *Future Shock*

"Tell me, and I will forget. Show me, and I may remember. Involve me, and I will understand."
-Confucius, Chinese Philosopher 550 B.C.

In writing the first draft of our letter to president elect Obama, I went to see my friend and principal Dr. Craig Rocha, and I queried him, "If there is one thing you'd want to tell the Change president, what would it be?" He leaned back in his chair and almost immediately spouted, "We need to move from so much standardization to more personalization."

I remember nodding my head in approval and quickly scribbling the short message down in my "Obama letter" notebook; my mind began reviewing the whirlwind of standardized tests and assessments bombarding administrators along with school communities especially since "No Child Left Behind." Clearly, the focus on test scores has smothered the world of education so much that any reform or improvement program or initiative must pass the litmus test of "testability." Education has gotten into a habit of reductively measurable results. Unless we can "count it," we do not consider it valid.

So I mailed my letter to the President; and I can sum my request of him -- based on my conversations with other educators -- in one sentence: "Students need less fact-based learning and more skills in independent, critical thinking." And, we need to balance our obsession with "standardized" tests with "personalization," regarding the individual humanity and character of our students.

When I taught my first class at the school where I now teach, a student named Ryan sat in the back, passively scoring "Cs" on all his work. My repeated attempts to get him to "jump higher" only taught me that he was exceptionally bright. He resisted my best efforts to engage him in greater rigor because as he continues to declare today, "It was boring and a waste of time." In spite of our young school's motto of "A new school for a new century," and our highly driven and conscientious efforts to be the best school for the post-modern era, we didn't or at least I didn't get it. We were boring to Ryan. He felt his intelligence and passions were not regarded enough.

Today, Ryan is a mastermind behind all of my school's technology. He is a creator and maintainer of a very complex "cloud" of servers, hard drives and miles and miles of cables and wires. The greatest irony is that Ryan currently ushers us, the faculty and staff (all his elders), gradually to fluency in his brave new world. He even refers to himself as a "native speaker" of technology. The bottom line with students like Ryan is that he was a natural critical thinker and creator. At home when schoolwork wasn't in his way, he would pour over tech reports and manuals of the Lennox operating system among many others. He would delve into the depths of the complex and rapidly evolving world of computer operating systems. He was growing his fluency, and becoming a native speaker of several technological dialects all the time assessing and evaluating which systems were effective and useful.

We need to invest more time teaching students how to think, not how to take standardized tests. What's more, when we consider what conclusions are drawn by educators from an "up" or "down" slide in scores - too often guesses, at best – we can also begin to appreciate the amount of energy, worry and precious time we spend on the "test" issue. Perhaps the most significant indictment of public education was published in 1983. *A Nation at Risk* found that many seventeen-year- olds could not draw inferences and write a persuasive essay. The report by the National Commission on Excellence rang loud and clear: set standards. That, in turn, set off a frenzy of testing among states.

We are imbalanced when we trouble over only what is discretely and reductively measurable. We operate too much in the left cerebral hemisphere. When we worry and fuss over these fact-based assessments, we disregard the whole realm of emotions, relationships and mentoring so important to education. Indeed, we lose our own human personhood as well. Victor Villasenor, author of <u>Rain of Gold</u> among other books, shared with me that students: "don't care what you know until they know that you care." The feelings of students are the ground upon which all learning succeeds or fails. Unless your students buy into the educational experience, unless they are engaged, motivated, unless their interest is piqued, you are speaking over their heads to dead air. Remembering the year the War of 1812 started is not being educated.

Yet, according to the Gates AP College Readiness Report of 2007: "For the most part, high stakes standardized tests require students to recall or recognize fragmented and isolated bits of information. Those that do contain performance tasks are severely limited in the time that task can take and in their breadth or depth. The tests rarely require students to exhibit proficiency in higher forms of cognition."

- Marzano, Dikering and McTighe

I train teachers and school staff often throughout the country, and although I experience the subtle cultural differences that make this a dynamic nation, I have come to recognize some great parallels among all the educators I meet. Most carry a deep fear. This fear has a few faces. For some their fear has the face of the challenging students we must teach. Others it is their administrator who has the frightening look. For most, though, the fear is of low scores on the state mandated "standardized test." Most of these educators, who came to teaching out of a deep moral desire of help others grow, are not as consumed with growing their craft or learning dynamic teaching or engaging in continuous, self-correcting improvement of their vocations. Too often they are eroded out of their moral purpose by the years of attention to the test. How could they easily maintain their primal idealism considering the shrill attention given to exam scores? Simply put, we spend an enormous amount of time, and vital human energy on tests and test results. That being said, assessments are vital to teachers, students, schools and communities. Tests are important.

The issue is balance; and since we tend to be a culture which is ruled, regulated and driven by the left-brain, we need some kind of kick in the head to begin balancing our collective approach to educating America – especially, as we become more and more culturally diverse. That is why I call this new balance "radical." We tend to have a preference for what we can count and that upon which we can easily place a numerical value. Tellingly, American doctors often tell stroke victims that they are "lucky" when the stroke occurs on the right side of their brain, because it's not the "important" side. In doing so these doctors illustrate our almost blinded love and familiarity with the linear-sequential, the countable, the "measurable." Yet, even Einstein recognized the limitations on this way of viewing the world. The foremost practitioner of the problem solving, whose Special Theory of Relativity came in a blinding flash of insight on a city bus, often questioned the linearity of the scientific method: "Not everything that can be counted counts, and not everything that counts can be counted." Lost in a storm of testing, we too often do not see what counts.

Recently, while talking to a group of teachers, making the case that helping students identify their "passion" in life is an important role of an educator, a teacher raised her hand and asked, "How could you measure that?" I responded, "By asking the student." We are indeed, so blinded by this measuring, we don't even consider a conversation as a valid form of assessment. We have been "Scan-Tronized" away from the myriad of assessments that are not strictly data based, and reductive. We are enthralled by these very discrete and overly simplistic methods of gaining feedback.

Once you have been around enough children and adults, especially in the world of education where we assume we know what intelligence is, you have to accept that the power and capacities of each human being are very hard to quantify. So many organic, non-mathematical variables affect intelligence and learning such as emotions, self-image, nutrition, culture, family, geography, time in history, not to mention the foundational beliefs within the teachers and students themselves. These very beliefs can result in the growth or stunting of a child's mind. Too often I still hear the words, "Some kids are just not gonna get it." When an educator entertains that stunted, foundational belief, I can guarantee that the student in question *won't* get it!

Spencer Kagan, internationally acclaimed researcher, trainer and author of more than 80 books argues that some of education's biggest problems result from disengagement. Simply stated, traditional instructional delivery systems fail to engage all students. Dr. Howard Gardner and his Multiple Intelligences and Sir Ken Robinson's ideas about the rich complexities of human creative powers both make much more complete and balanced sense than do SAT or standardized scores. Even the thought that a student has "scores" assigned to him/her seems laughable – in a terrifying way. Educators and their factoid tests appear as players of checkers - far from the three-dimensional chessboard that is the real classroom. In my presentations to other educators, I like to pose the following challenge that illustrates the trouble that black-and-white grades and scoring poses.

First take on this temporary role: you are a ninth-grade math teacher at the end of the term, grading "summative assessments or "FINALS" as we refer to them. Oh, and also consider that the standard for the lessons which conclude with this FINAL is "Decimal Points." Are you ready to perform your task as a 9th -grade math grader? Below is the problem and the student's answer is next to it. So you don't have to do all the work, just know that the numbers that the student calculated and wrote down are all correct; the multiplication, addition, the "carry the this " and "carry the that" are all done properly. The final answer has all of the correct numbers in the correct places. However, there is no decimal point. For whatever reason, it was left out. Your responsibility is to score this problem for 0 points to a total possible of 9 points. Consider this problem then score it as a good teacher.

$$
\begin{array}{r}
8.267 \\
11.35 \\
\times \underline{\hspace{2cm}} \\
41335 \\
24801 \\
8267 \\
8267 \\
\hline
9383045
\end{array}
$$

The entire math is done correctly – well over twenty separate computations are all correct, but the decimal is missing from the final answer. Remember that the "standard" for this unit test is "decimal points."

This activity originates from Dr. Richard Curwin, who wrote <u>*Discipline with Dignity*</u>. He had over 100 teachers fired up about this issue. In fact, they got so upset about other teachers' philosophies and decision-making that several shouting matches broke out. Since attending Dr Curwin's training, I performed this activity where I show a PowerPoint slide of a mutli-stage math problem. I ask the same question and, basically, get the same diversity of responses and upset the same numbers in my audiences.

The most common grade given in both Curwin's workshop and mine is 6 points out of nine. Next in frequency is a score of 7 points out of 9. There generally is a fair number who vote to give the problem a "0" points. In this "0" score group are a large number of math teachers. What's interesting is that those in the majority that give the student a 6 or 7 rarely have a similar rationale for their decisions. Even teachers that agree on the number of points, completely disagree about <u>why</u> they give the score.

On the other hand, when I question those who have scored the problem a "0," there often is unanimity in the rationale for their scoring. It usually boils down to a declaration that this is math, that there is a right answer, and everything short of that is wrong. Often, the presentation of this reasoning is accompanied by a low "Booing" or other sounds of clear verbal consternation throughout the meeting hall – probably, from those who always hated math, their childhood math teacher, and the whole right/wrong paradigm.

I usually defend those who have the courage to give the problem zero points with the story of a family going on vacation in an SUV. If a kid, like the one who forgot the decimal point, was an engineer and builder of any of the bridges that this family happened to drive over, he might be responsible for their deaths. When it comes to building bridges, automobiles, aircraft or even chairs, precision does matter. Decimal points matter. There are consequences for imprecision in many aspects of our culture. This is magnified many times if you consider banking or medical computations.

So the "zero-point" teachers are right. Right? As you can imagine, there is always a lively debate during these sessions which often result in many teachers folding their arms across their chests in a defensive certainty. At this moment, I point out to them -- I admit with more than a little secret satisfaction -- that a whole room full of teachers cannot agree on how to score ONE LITTLE OLE MATH PROBLEM with anything approaching unanimity! If some of our nation's most highly educated professionals can't agree on one the most objective assessments in the world of education -- a single math problem – how can we? What many teachers and educational leaders fail to get is that there are no ULTIMATE easy answers.

We avoid accepting the natural and organic messiness that always exists in this world of learning. Most importantly, there are no ABSOLUTE right answers. There are only answers that we argue for and ultimately agree upon. Between the conceptual world of what is right and the messy reality of the human organism, we must struggle for a best response and a best answer. There is a great deal of difference between "the best" and the "right." The best answer is arrived at collaboratively, and the right answer comes from a dogmatist without debate.

Next, I single out the teacher who gave the student a "0" on the math problem and pose a new question: "What if the student put the decimal point in the correct place, but made other errors in addition and the answer had two wrong numbers in the final answer? To this question, the "zero" point teachers usually state that, "If the answer is wrong, it's wrong." Remember they gave NO CREDIT for any of the work that happened to be correct in the first place.

Then I state that if they believe in not rewarding the correct addition and multiplication and that is why they originally gave the zero score, was it not double jeopardy to punish the same multiplication and addition if it is done incorrectly – even if the decimal is in the right place? In other words they did not reward points when the other parts of the problem were correct. But they would punish the child for getting the very same parts of the problem wrong. They would punish, but not reward. This point generally elicits confused faces and exasperation.

At this point, someone usually volunteers that their school has a math rubric to resolve these kinds of debates about scoring problems. These rubrics are often described as some sort of supreme authority, kind of like this department-agreed-upon rubric that has been chiseled in stone or brought down from the mountain. I offer that their rubric or system of grading may be exhaustively researched and the result of many faculty meetings, but that fact doesn't necessarily make their effort objective. Is the rubric universal? Can it be applied to a Louisiana State school or a school in rural Minnesota? Or how about in China where they do this math thing better than we do, apparently by teaching fewer objectives? Besides isn't it too often the case that one or two loud, extroverted teachers with clout or tenure decide most of these "committee-agreed upon" rubrics? How many of these big decisions are actually made by very few people?

Now, to complicate this grading or assessment problem even more, how would you grade a science project, an essay, or a short essay in a written history exam? How about a group project with a written assignment and an oral presentation? All of these contain many more layers of complexity than our simple little math problem. All this is to say that the enormous worry time and energy that educators labor under for the sake of state, national or local standardized testing is suspect in its overall usefulness -- at best. At its worst, it is a growing impediment to the mission of shaping young minds. For instance, for many years the State tests were not even designed with the State standards in mind. Also, it is a crap shoot for each school to guess just what standards will be given most emphasis for any particular year. Plus, if you have very many disenfranchised, at risk or emerging language students in the testing group, these state testing instruments amount to little more than unsupportive torture.

The point is that standardized tests have many problems and mixed meanings for many of us in education. Again, it bears repeating that some form of testing is ABSOLUTELY NECESSARY IN EDUCATION. Our problem is how we simultaneously worship, fear and regard the standardized tests that are currently in vogue. Much of this standardization is politically driven by policy makers who have absolutely no clue about education other than getting a score which is like the math problem. The power we give these instruments truly saps too much energy that could be better directed.

At most schools in California - and this is repeated in other states across the nation – four whole weeks out of a school year are specifically devoted to testing by various State instruments. Posters are made; meetings are held; testing strategies are disseminated; and tutorials are held. At some schools I have visited, students who do poorly on these tests must spend all day, every period in math, math support, math tutorial and remediation. For the sake of the schools' collective score, many schools morph into monsters that condemn their students who are struggling the most in the very subjects in which they have been struggling the most. Talk about happy childhood memories for the yearbook! And what happens to these students' progress in their other areas of study?

Yes, this left-brain, practice-makes-perfect approach to education makes some sense and has a certain historical currency. But there is an enormous imbalance being created by making at-risk or otherwise-struggling students do math all day long. This approach ignores the emotional state of already emotionally fragile individuals and completely discounts what we have learned about motivating students positively and other elements essential to long-lasting learning. It's one-dimensional and archaic. It speaks to only one aspect of the Triune Brain – the one least developed in a teenager.

Look at it from the child's perspective. He or she must feel they have been thrust into one of those horror movies where the maniac discovers your greatest fear – rats, snakes, listening to the Carpenters -- and then condemns you to endure it for a whole school semester. These are the sort of situations and school-based decisions that result in the 30%, 40% or even 50% dropout rates across our nation. In our frenzied worship of and unquestioning reverence for these tests, we have lost sight of the human element, the human child in the seats right in front of us. The emotions, the young psyches, the personal stories they are, and are living don't count.

We have to create a new balance between testing and the human element. Carl Jung recognized this when he said, "An understanding heart is everything in a teacher, and cannot be esteemed highly enough; one looks back with appreciation to the brilliant teachers, but with gratitude to those who touched our human feeling. The curriculum is so much necessary raw material, but warmth is the vital element for the growing plant and soul of the child."

This balance will be hard to achieve. Our American culture values the measurable so much that we are accustomed to this paradigm in an annoyingly crude sort of way. In addition, there is a hidden profit motive in all this testing. For example, during the 1990s, the billion-dollar testing industry pushed California statewide assessments away from using a variety of "authentic" assessments or demanding tasks, such as applying or evaluating information in a short essay- justified response or portfolios. Sir Ken Robinson says in his book _The Element,_ that we are "enthralled "by certain beliefs and routines." We believe that the status quo of education is "just the way it's supposed to be." We are so enthralled that we won't even question the oft-repeated mantra "is it measurable?"

We need to question when districts and schools spend inordinate amounts of time, energy and treasure on posters, training seminars - all so we can see if our scores went up. Again, across the country, a common anxiety indigenous to American education is the fear voiced on all levels of state, local and school-wide tests. Teachers will complain, "My principal is all charged up about raising scores," or administrators will bark, "I've got to get my teachers concerned" about getting higher test scores. We rarely hear this same level of energy committed to creating better teaching methodologies or improving the learning environment in a class. I have heard teachers share their fear of losing their jobs over scores, but I have never heard a single teacher fear losing their job because they failed to foster critical reasoning in students or failing to inspire or motivate them.

Now, to clarify, all assessment instruments or tests have gifts and liabilities associated with them – and, under the current educational environment (2011), they are mostly liabilities. In addition, all tests, even the best-constructed ones, contain at least some questionable elements. We all know that tests are necessary and useful tools for the student, teacher, parents, and government. We educators can use them to determine, to a certain degree, what students learned from us. These tools can give us a partial picture of the effects our teaching had, so we can self-assess our own effectiveness and that of the school structures and culture as well. Depending on the effectiveness and reliability of the tests or assessments we can gain a great deal of insight into what the kids know. We have to keep in mind that some of what the students show on the test may have been learned before we taught them, so again the full picture is still fuzzy.

Most telling is the fact that most standardized state tests, generally ask for only factoids or data points with maybe a few rudimentary formulas – all stuff that is easily and often forgotten by students. The College Board's exams created by the Educational Testing Service (ETS) are relentlessly researched, tried and tested, and reconsidered -- at great cost to the College Board. They spend FAR more time and treasure creating and improving their Advanced Placement and SAT tests than the best teachers in America do for their own tests and assessments. Still, their best efforts come under constant and continued criticism that they fail to show many a students' gifts and powers. They are also criticized for being class or culturally biased, gender biased, and only being capable of showing what a student knows for one moment in time.

A growing number of higher institutions are beginning to question the validity of their tests, including Bowdoin College – the first to remove the SAT from admissions requirements as well as Lafayette College in Pennsylvania. Even the giant University of California system of colleges has been considering making their own test to replace the College Board's best effort. The sad fact remains that our unbalanced perception of all tests diminishes our efforts at teaching in a way, which results in rich and lasting learning. In his "Time" magazine article, "Should SATs Matter?" John Cloud notes, "Aside from that class inequality, the test's failure to measure anything meaningful also meant that kids were spending a lot of time fretting over pedagogical phantoms at the expense of real learning."

Data and what we call "Info-bits" are lost unless continuously used or unless associated with something meaningful in the student's mind. William Dagget, a noted speaker on all issues educational, noted at a speech to several hundred teachers of which I was one, that a study was done on the East Coast where 1,200 valedictorians and salutatorians -- the first and second highest GPA-rated students -- were all given a ninth-grade final exam, which they had all taken at the end of their Freshman year in high school. Now, guess what percentage of these "best" students passed the test that they took a few years before?

Drum roll, please: Only 15% passed a test they took a few years before. So what? Considering we are talking about the "best" students of their generation, what did they really learn in school and what do they really know? These kids obviously know how to play the school game. They're unquestionably bright – the best and the brightest, if you will -- have great study skills, great memories, know how to manage their time, and certainly can retain facts long enough to pass our tests. But we also must face the fact that they don't remember much of what they are taught - at least, not the stuff we test them on. So what does this say about the kind of rote memory measured in standardized tests? What is the long-term value of these kinds of facts when they are not connected to other aspects of the human mind -- the emotional or social aspects of the total being, perhaps?

WHAT DO WE DO, THEN? *The hard facts about the soft arts of education*

What we can conclude that it is essential that we move towards a more holistic and individual-centric approach to the classroom. To quote our AVID letter to president Obama, we want to move "from standardization to personalization," so that our approach to teaching and leading youth is more balanced. Let's not try to cram all-shaped pegs into the same-shaped hole. This isn't a new idea; it's actually rather ancient reaching all the way back to Socrates.

Most education before the industrial age was based on relationship and long-term mentoring which we call apprenticeship. You learned with someone, hands on, and what you learned had immediate practical application for what you did or produced on the job. In most cases your apprenticeship helped support you or your family. Education was relevant and had a specific and rather immediate impact on your survivability and prosperity. Education was, at its core, social, and essential to your family, town, tribe and culture. This is how knowledge was passed on reaching all the way back to the earliest days of human culture when older tribe members passed on the tribe's technology and customs to younger members for the mutual survivability of all. Education was important --literally, a matter of life and death – and an activity whose importance was obvious to both the teacher and student.

Lev Vygotsky, a rather famous Russian linguist and educator developed the idea of a "zone of proximal development." In summary, this zone of development is that amount of learning that the child can accomplish alone when given a task <u>with</u> the wise intermittent involvement of the teacher. Just as the pupil reaches an impasse, the teacher gives the next new information the child needs to grow. This "zone" is where teacher and pupil sort of waltz together into an accelerated pace of learning, and it is highly differentiated or suited to the needs and gifts of the child. This zone is also radically ideal: one teacher, one student.

What's important to note is that Vygotzky's zone model speaks to the reality of the human condition, revealing the social-relational groundwork upon which real learning has been based. It's all about relationships – between teacher and student, student and student and student and extended family. Ken Robinson, in one of his talks we attended, asked the audience what the absolute bare essentials of education were? He told us to imagine tearing away all the unions, contracts, buildings, sports fields, computers etc. What's left? "You have a teacher and a learner," he said -- and even that may be too rigid because sometimes the teacher must become the learner. So at the <u>core</u>, teaching occurs within and because of the medium of the relationship.

Thus it is that we issue a battle cry to American Education: "relationships first, tests later." Assessments and learning intertwine. In fact several studies have shown the power of relationships on learning AND test scores. There is a reading program referenced in Robinson's book "The Element" where seniors in a retirement home are helping children learn to read. The result is multifold: The students get to read and talk to and share stories with the elderly and vice versa. Students are getting one-to-one social history lessons as a result; the students are out-performing the children in the rest of the district on standardized reading tests and "70% are learning the program at age five, reading at third-grade level. Aside from the testable academic elements, the elderly tutors at "Grace Living Center" have cut back or stopped many of their medications. These fortunate elderly volunteers now have a reason "to get up in the morning."

One study I remember reading a few years back concluded that new learning would be vivid and long lasting if the learner knows the teacher and cares for him or her. This study gave as an example a grandmother teaching a complicated needlepoint knot to a grandchild. Even the proximity of the grandmother to the child increased memory. In this profession of education I worry that we, too often, see ourselves as "professional," which denotes a distance from those being taught, a lack of familiarity and emotional connection – emotional connectivity being a potential pitfall for teachers nowadays. Still, we need to see more human emotional reality in the classroom.

If we think about the professionals in our lives that have touched us or connected with us as people -- those who have an opportunity to get to know us and our unique strengths and challenges -- they have usually done so when they have crossed the professional "line" and become human beings. For example, as a teacher, I will assign students to synthesize a reading, assigning students to write a creative or inventive poem about the reading. I too, will write a poem and read it to my class so as to share and connect with them by also experiencing the process of the assignment.

We need to see the social element of the classroom as important along with the academic. Indeed, developing a "social contract" with the students is a powerful way to set behavioral and relational expectations with the input of the students. Even many private as well as governmental organizations today are now utilizing "social contracts" in order to improve the collegial nature of the workplace. Since many of the best ways to foster student engagement are collaborative, appropriate behaviors need to be defined and followed by the whole class as well as smaller groups with it. Importantly, the "social contract" is created by direct input from the students themselves which creates more personal investment. Too many of American youths are fuzzy on the idea of *graciousness*, and the social contract helps clarify important social interaction norms that are supportive of team and group learning.

In response to those, like former Secretary of Education William Bennet who considered paying attention to the social and personal elements of learning as "soft," it bears stating that this shift is NOT an EITHER/OR shift. We are not advocating the eradication of rigor or exams or rules or standards. We are begging for a balance that asks as much of educators human, social/emotional selves as it does of their efforts to standardize and assess. Keep in mind that high scores can be attached to how the teacher succeeds at MOTIVATING AND INSPIRING kids to do more and better in school.

Mark Twain, whose books are read in classrooms of varying grade levels across this nation, did not attend high school. And I imagine his oft-quoted saying that he "never let [his] schooling interfere with [his] education" was the result of too much boring rote memorization and un-engaging teaching. Too many people feel like Twain. One of his most deadly quotes about the endemic failure of education at his time was, "Education and soap are not as sudden as a massacre, but they are more deadly in the long run."

Many of us in education are blindly settling for the status quo --first, because the system is what we have always known and, second, because we fear change. Many teachers go to work disenchanted, hurt and without the spark that originally inspired them. Schooling has indeed been "deadly in the long run." Many teachers have shared their frustrations with Gary and me, how they feel that the system and our leadership are out of whack. Well, we know that change <u>can</u> happen. That improvement can begin in a classroom – then a department, then a school and beyond. We need to spark more creative approaches in the classroom – creativity in service of agreed-upon standards. Places like "Grace Living Center" are possible.

As previously noted, Victor Villasenior, author of <u>Rain of Gold,</u> among many other books, has stated, "You don't teach Math or English, you teach children, and they won't care what you know until they know that you care." In his lectures, he has a core conviction that we are all geniuses, but that many of us have not had our genius recognized. His friend and mentor, psychologist Dr. Bill Cartwright, told me that he has one essential goal as a teacher: "light the fire in the belly of my students." Lighting a passion or mentoring someone into their genius may not be easily measured, but I have hopes of creating such an assessment. This assessment may be as simple as asking a student if I have helped them find their genius or geniuses.

Both Robinson and Villasenior do a similar activity when they speak across the country. They ask the audience to rate or rate themselves. Victor asks people to raise their hands if they believe they are geniuses. Robinson asks them to rate their intelligence on a 1-10 scale, with 10 being the top. Both Villasenior and Robinson state that the audience routinely under-reports their intelligence or denies that they are geniuses. Victor says that children will raise their hands much more than adults do. Is school at fault for this? Is school today "more deadly in the long run"? Robinson states that the problem is our narrow definition of intelligence. He states, "I'm convinced that taking the definition of intelligence for granted is one of the main reasons why so many people underestimate their true intellectual abilities and fail to find their element."

Robinson's concept of the "element" is much akin to Villasenior's idea of "genius": it is the work or activity for which you have specific gifts and passion. For Victor, his genius, among several, is writing stories. Dyslexic and having never completed college, he has published several novels, screenplays and, at this writing, HBO is serializing his award winning book <u>Rain of Gold.</u> Victor never did well on standardized tests. Yet, he has changed the lives of millions. Robison offers a simple test for finding if you are in your element or passion: "Time passes differently" and "when people are in their element, they connect with something fundamental to their sense of identity, purpose, and well-being."

So, why isn't a student's passion a central question in teacher training? Why isn't the task of helping students find and make meaning and connecting to the teacher central to our tasks as educators? You can get great test scores AND light the bellies of children. And yes, every teacher can increase their capacity at connecting and inspiring students even though it may or may not be measurable. Consider what the greatest mind of the 20th century said about what counts aside from numbers and measurable values. Again, as Albert Einstein pointed out, "Not everything that can be counted, counts, and not everything that counts can be counted."

Active Minds

Along with addressing the core reality that students are human beings *first* before they are students or learners, we must engage their growing minds more. Education must become more than Twain's caustic soap. The 19th century model of the classroom is visually represented by rows of desks and children silently doing bookwork. This is the very sort of learning that Twain and many of us can easily recall as the boring nature of schooling. Those valedictorians that forgot the facts in their ninth grade exams attest to the ineffectiveness of this "industrial model" of the classroom. As Mark Twain quipped, "Many public school children seem to know only two dates – 1492 and the fourth of July; and as a rule, they don't know what happened on either occasion."

We need to adopt what Sir Ken Robinson calls the "agriculture model" of education where the teacher as "farmer" sets up the environment and facilitates the learning. Dr. Robinson uses the Michelin Guide as an example of the agricultural approach. The Michelin guides are probably the most respected guides and judgers of restaurants and food around the planet. They use a system of three stars as their "grades" for particular restaurants. The judges consider five criteria for awarding stars: quality, flavor, personality, value, and consistency. The manner and approach of the restaurants is up to them and their own creative choices. The results ARE NOT specifically dictated by the Michelin guide. Freedom of imagination and discipline are the key ingredients to attaining the highest ranking.

This model allows choice by the student individually or in groups to attain high grades. This paradigm is looser in nature than a controlled class of children where their every move is circumscribed by the educational establishment out of a fear of "chaos." This approach does accept a little risking by students; and this, in turn, is risky for the educator. An example of this new modality is project-based or problem-based learning. In both cases, rubrics are set and students are allowed some freedom in responding. Developed at a Canadian medical school, Problem-Based Learning places Students in small groups so they can investigate and analyze problems/scenarios, an element that speaks to our mammalian brains.

Using an organizer, this process involves 1) identifying the FACTS in the problem/scenario; 2) generating (un-criticized) the student IDEAS about the scenario/problem, identifying just "what is the problem?" 3) Finally identifying the things must LEARN in order to test their hypotheses (ideas).

This approach is also school-wide at the sister schools of California Polytechnic University at both San Luis Obispo and Pomona. Both of these universities are within the California State University system and, interestingly, have agricultural origins. Both schools share a genesis that began in 1900 with a philosophy called "Learning by Doing." This approach has now evolved to be called "Theorypractice." Both of these schools have record level success at post-education employment because industries know that these schools immerse their students in hands-on, real-world problem solving and project creation. They also utilize a great deal of teaming and collaboration in their curricula. For example, students learn about the chemistry and physics of hydraulic concrete; then, later that day or week, they meet as a team with the goal of designing and building a concrete canoe which they must race at year's end against other like students from across the country. As Dr. William Edwards Deming, American business professor and author stated, "You don't just learn knowledge; you have to create it. Get in the driver's seat, don't just be a passenger. You have to contribute to it or you don't understand it."

Whereas we as a nation used to actively engage students more in schools, especially after the Soviet Union launched the Sputnik satellite on October 4, 1957, we have slid from this tendency. For example, at one time, Connecticut had one of the highest-rated state testing programs in the nation, mixing multiple choice and essays. On a fifth grade reading test the students are asked to "read about a popular game in Uganda, and then they were asked to write an essay "comparing the African game with a game they play at their school." Imagine how much more creative and complex this text item is as compared with what we ask of children on the current factoid-laden standardized exams. Furthermore, Connecticut requires students in secondary level tests to design and carry out a lab experiment, record the results, and answer questions about it.

These test items are much more multi-faceted, complex and engaging. Authentic and creative assessments are in danger of passing away because they cost more. NCLB will only fund enough for cheaper and faster, machine-graded tests. Testing companies charge fifty cents to grade a multiple-choice test, but they will charge five dollars for an essay. State and national resources, as well as tight regulatory deadlines imposed by NCLB, threaten to erode these gold standard tests – tests that illustrate the idea of Radical Balance. Indeed, Massachusetts Institute of Technology Professor Emeritus Seymour Papert calls it this more dynamic approach to learning, "Constructionism which means learning by making something. LEGO is an example - writing computer programs is an example - painting is an example. And what you learn in the process of doing sinks in much deeper. Its roots go deeper into the subsoil of the mind than anything anybody can tell you." The problem is we do not teach this way in most American schools, private, charter or otherwise.

Besides, the Chinese are literally laughing at us. Dr. Jonathan Plucker of Indiana University recently toured a number of schools in Shanghai and Beijing. His experiences were noted in a recent article in Newsweek,

"He was amazed by a boy who, for a class science project, rigged a tracking device for his moped with parts from a cell phone. When faculty of a major Chinese university asked Plucker to identify trends in American education, he described our focus on standardized curriculum, rote memorization, and nationalized testing. "After my answer was translated, they just started laughing out loud," Plucker says. "They said, 'You're racing toward our old model. But we're racing to your model as fast as we can."

Two major forces are converging that we need to acknowledge: One, the 19th century approach to the classroom does not align with how the brain best attends, processes, retains and recalls information. And, Two, Our "new normal" of the 21st century is a non-symmetrical workplace environment of continued change which requires multi-disciplined, creative, problem solving to survive. While traditional instructional methods of the past may have worked for the past century, they fail to produce skills necessitated by the present and future world environment. We need to revisit our familiar past, and do it quickly. We must make creativity a top educational standard, and learn to balance our approach to educating. As is illustrated in the following diagram, we need to balance personalization, standardization and active learning:

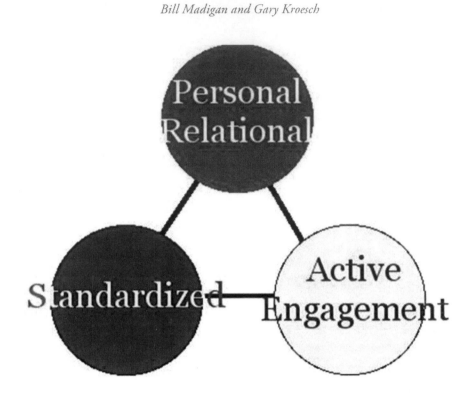

Daniel Pink author of A Whole New Mind and Thomas Freidman, a three-time winner of the Pulitzer Prize and editorial columnist for the New York Times offer a great definition for the concept of *Radical Balance*:

FRIEDMAN: I'll give you one of my favorite examples: Rainforest Math. There's so much one can learn from the laws of nature--not just biology, but Einstein, Newton, physics. And you drive both environmentalism and you drive math. So it's those kinds of intersections that are going to produce the most innovative students.

PINK: So how do we bring that into the system? There's team teaching, integrating the arts into the curriculum, writing across subject areas. What else?

FRIEDMAN: I think you've got to force it a little like Georgia Tech did and say: "You are going to study computing, and you are going to study screenwriting." Then the assignment in the class is: Write an online play with what you've learned.

PINK: That makes sense. Instruction in the subject matter areas, but then leave the execution to the students. And give them a fair amount of autonomy along the way.

FRIEDMAN: Right. The assignment can be: "Mash these two together."

****

For Further Exploration

Radical Balance

Publications:

Brockman, M. (2009). *What's next: dispatches on the future of science.* New York, NY: Vintage Books.
[This book is a collection of readings illustrating cutting edge scientific discoveries with projections of their effects on our future.]

Kagan, S. (1994). *Kagan cooperative learning* (2nd ed.). San Clemente, CA: Kagan Cooperative Learning.
[Practical structures for teambuilding and group learning.]

Pausch, R., & Zaslow, J. (2008). *The last lecture.* New York, NY: Hyperion Books.
[This book contains advice from this Carnegie Mellon computer science Professor on achieving your dreams.]

Pink, D. (2005). *A Whole New Mind.* New York, NY: Riverhead Books.
[This book illustrates the need to utilize the whole brain, especially the creative capacities.]

Robinson, K. (2009). *The element: how finding your passion changes everything.* New York City, NY: Penguin Group.
[The author demonstrates the need to discover our passions for our sake and the sake of mankind.]

Websites

Advancement Via Individual Determination. (2010). *AVID- Decades of college dreams.* Retrieved from http://www.avid.org
[Their mission is to close the achievement gap by preparing ALL students for college readiness and success in a global society.]

Buck Institute for Education. (2011). Buck Institute for Education: Project based learning. Retrieved from http://www.bie.org/
[Buck institute for education is dedicated to improving 21st century teaching and learning through "project-based" learning.]

California State Polytechnic University, Pomona. (2011). *Mission, values, and vision.* Retrieved from http://www.csupomona.edu/mission.php
[Cal Poly Pomona's vision and mission statements which aim, "to advance learning and knowledge by linking theory and practice."]

Landsberger, J. (2011). *Problem-based learning.* Study Guides and Strategies. Retrieved from http://www.studygs.net/pbl.htm
[This is a resource for "Problem based learning" where learning becomes active through the discovery to solve problems.]

Pausch, R. (2008). *The last lecture -- Randy Pausch.* YouTube. Retrieved from http://www.youtube.com/watch?v=e_2NAM4jWbw

5

What We Need to Face About Gender, Sexual Orientation and Sexual Desire and the Classroom

The source of all life and knowledge is in man and woman, and the source of all living is in the interchange and the meeting and mingling of these two: man-life and woman-life, man-knowledge and woman-knowledge, man-being and woman-being.

D. H. Lawrence *(1885-1930) English writer.*

It's the rare neuroscientist or neurobiologist who will admit that there are any striking differences between males and females. This is usually for political or overly cautious reasons. Yet, as you leave the refined arenas of research labs or academic journals, differences between the sexes are many and patently obvious. Psychologists and sociologists recognize them as do teachers, educators and parents. As noted in the chapter on the brain, adolescent boys do engage the environment more physically than the typical girl. So do infant boys, for that matter. At the same time, girls do tend to experience more emotional variability – emotional ups and downs, if you will.

Both of these generalized traits alone are powerful enough to require that they be treated differently. Anything less is a disservice to the child;

and a formula for failure in the classroom. This has nothing to do with treating them equitably, which is a given. It speaks only to the need to recognize the different outlooks on the world that teenage boys and girls have and to speak to them "in a language they will understand." Not to paint this with too broad a brush; not every situation requires different modalities. It merely goes to the point that the educator needs to take account of the uniqueness of each sex as well as of individuals and to communicate with each appropriately.

There are exceptions and an individual boy or girl often will require more specialized treatment specific to the situation. But, in general, acknowledging gender traits can be helpful in classroom management, our choices of tactics for active learning and "reaching" the child – not to mention that the teacher who doesn't acknowledge that emotions and gender differences are real and present in the school setting may be insensitive to the signals that students give off.

Who among us is going to be comfortable sitting in a chair for six hours a day, day in and day out, listening to lectures? How quickly does that get old? For one thing, it speaks to only one aspect of our Triune Brain. We want to engage the whole brain whenever possible. "Whole body" learning utilizes dances, plays, debates, and physical symbolic motion among other kinesthetic learning activities. Getting kids up and out of their chairs periodically is a good idea -- and not just for boys. Girls enjoy the social aspect of these activities and all people learn better when multiple neural pathways are created which support the learning. Activities that engage our Reptilian and Mammalian brain stems along with the neo-cortex reinforce one another. Movement combined with chanting creates still more neural pathways, and when this is done in pairs or small groups, the social nature of the learning activity is more engaging still. These kinds of activities create a more pleasurable learning experience that engages the physical, social and emotional aspects of the individual that creates a context for information and, therefore, greater, longer memory.

With teen females having a tendency toward more pronounced emotional changes, the idea of mentoring becomes beneficial. Making connections with learners has always been an important educational goal and is supported by reams of research. Teaching girls that they have a general tendency towards emotional changes during the teen years, and that they are not alone in this regard is a powerful form of metacognition for them as well as the mentor. It frees the introverted among them from the feeling that they are the oddball or strange – fitting-in being a primary motivation among teens. Then too, letting them know that you will accept and support them, that you appreciate them for their individuality and that emotional energy can be channeled for advancement also is important to recognize -- for both student and mentor.

This is not to say that just any kind of emotional expression is acceptable. There are limits and the limits must be communicated both implicitly and explicitly. But children need to know that, no matter what they do, they will still be cared about and will be accepted as human beings. Acceptance is very high on every teenager's hierarchy of needs. Of course, there is a line that the mentor must walk and he or she must be careful in how support is expressed as we'll explore later in the chapter.

Educational leaders may need to work on being less emotionally reactive themselves, so that they are more capable of responding appropriately. The more emotionally volatile a person is, the fewer solutions seem occur because the neo-cortex and its creative capacities are severely diminished by a virtually screaming amygdala. When you are upset, your capacity to respond sensibly or weigh the factors in a complex problem is severely limited.

Concomitant with a girl's labyrinth of feelings is a generalized "fuzziness" in the sense of self and/or self-possession. Their egos are in flux. Certainly, they are capable of very assertive bouts at times -- ironically, to a greater degree among females who tend to have greater self-doubt and less solid or consistent sense of who they are. All humans seem to have a tendency to talk louder and more forcefully the less sure they are of their argument. There are many possible causes for females' lack of confidence, but among them are an overarching concern for the opinions of their peers and adults alike and a growing need for supportive relationships with both groups. These can have positive outcomes, but they also could tend to muddy the waters of a still-forming ego if the proper balance isn't struck.

Coursing through teen bloodstreams are a host of hormones that prompt for social interactions and a generalized desire to share feelings with others. This can have many dimensions. For example, girls with higher amounts of the "trust hormone," Oxytocin, tend to ache for connection with others. This can have both good and bad outcomes for the inexperienced, impressionable and vulnerable teen. Regardless, this tendency leaves them less assertive and more self-correcting in the academic classroom – that also exhibits as self doubt. Unless the environment is supportive and encouraging, fewer girls ask questions and take part in discussion. Thus, effort needs to be expended to mitigate the negative outcomes and reward the positive behaviors prompted by this hormone mix.

There is a growing trend towards "gender schools" where the sexes are segregated in math and science classes. South Carolina has adopted a single-gender model for all middle schools over the next five years. It will be interesting to see if this effort will result in benefits for both or either of the two sexes, especially given the vast differences we are beginning to learn about their adolescent brains.

Preliminary attempts at this single gender classroom have shown that girls benefit the most from the arrangement. Females coming from poverty show this improvement extends to girls of all socio-economic strata. Self reporting by the girls suggests that girls feel more comfortable in girls' only classes. Again their reluctance to compete with boys may be the issue here. Girls also have been shown to have a greater capacity at group or cooperative learning and have a greater facility at communication in those groups. This is central to the success of problem-based or project-based learning.

In addition, some educators suggest that removing the sexual tension and drama connected to it leaves room for greater focus on learning. To check this belief out, I asked a few classes of students recently what they thought would be the benefits of single gender classes, and the most common answer was a reduction of "drama." Students would worry less about who looks the hottest today; who's "talking" to whom; even who is wearing what clothes. One student said they thought that a less sexually charged environment would result in less intense focus on "looks." Learning would have less competition. Growing brains would hold more priority that perhaps growing biceps or breasts.

Females have been improving their general success in school as of late. They are taking more advanced classes. They also attend college at a higher rate than males, reversing an ancient trend, and they are enrolled in larger numbers in graduate programs as well. With this in mind, a sort of synergy is building for even more females to succeed as more female role models are available to mentor and inspire others to follow. At this writing, 57% of college students are women, and if the trends over the last thirty years continue, woman will account for two-thirds of the college student body by 2020.

What this may mean for the future of the public school or the corporate boardroom can only be guessed at. Will the face of education become even more female in gender? What will that mean when most teachers are already female? Should we work for a greater balance of genders, let alone race? Will boys sense even more alienation as the world gradually grows more female professionals and leaders with advanced degrees?

What about the boys? For the last 20 years their educational numbers have been in general decline as compared to their sisters. In his article in Esquire article titled, *The Problem with Boys . . . is actually a problem with men,* Tom Chiarella says,

But here's the deal if you are a boy in this country right now:

You're twice as likely as a girl to be diagnosed with an attention-deficit or learning disorder. You're more likely to score worse on standardized reading and writing tests. You're more likely to be held back in school. You're more likely to drop out of school. If you do graduate, you're less likely to go to college. If you do go to college, you will get lower grades and, once again, you will be less likely to graduate. You'll be twice as likely to abuse alcohol, and until you are twenty-four, you are five times as likely to kill yourself. You are more than sixteen times as likely to go to prison.

In the following chart from the U.S. Census Bureau we can appreciate these disparities between males and females:

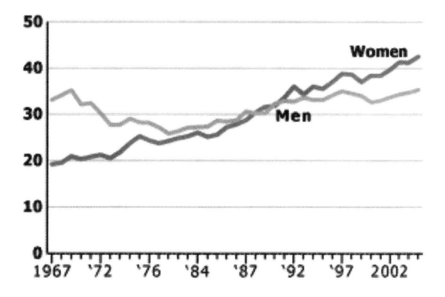

Actually, men have experienced little overall change in their rates of college enrollment from the peak around 1970. Obviously, the glass ceiling is broken. This is true across racial and cultural lines as well. Indeed, with women of color, especially blacks and Hispanics, gender enrollment is even more pronounced. Women enrolled in colleges in southern states enjoy the greatest gap in enrollment with their male counterparts. In Arkansas, there are 250 African-American women enrolled for every 100 black males. As illustrated in the chart below, all minority females are succeeding above their brothers. So the data shows that men aren't really worse off educationally, if you look at their college attendance rates compared with past years. Yet, women are doing better in all grades. Perhaps, the answer is that males are not doing worse so much as the women are really taking advantage of their new voices and freedoms.

However valuable it may be to have single gender classrooms, the adult- professional communities of the school site or district office ought to be gender balanced. Considering this evolution of genders, and that the research community is in general agreement that woman and men process the world differently in some important ways, we do need to work towards a greater parity of gender presence on campus and the administration. Girl students need both male and female role models, as do boys. In addition, decision making and collaborative problem solving by teacher teams and school districts will improve with the synergy resultant from both gender's voices. Conscious effort ought to be expended in creating balanced teams as often as possible. This is of course true in student groups and collaboration

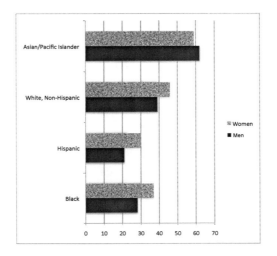

Sexual orientation and the classroom

Although we Americans don't usually discuss sex, sexuality, desire or even the idea of self-control very often or very meaningfully, we do have strong visceral feelings about male and female roles as well as how and what sex is or ought to be.

Gone are the days "when boys were boys and girls were girls." Now girls wear pants, play sports, talk back, and declare sexual harassment. Title IX has challenged many of those who see boys' sports as the "real' sports. Gender roles have shifted but, in many ways, stayed the same. Dishes are still washed by women by a wide margin in American homes; shopping, cleaning the house and general nurturing of the young is still, predominately, a female role. Certainly, there are higher percentages of men doing these roles than in the recent past. Yet, the majority still follows various traditional expectations.

What is new and is increasingly accepted are "boys who are girls" in many traditional ways. Some boys have lisping, sweet feminine sounding voices. Some males may express themselves non-verbally with what are often regarded degradingly as "limp-wrested" hand gestures that were once the manner of some women and few, if any, men. Now, more men do have these mannerisms, and many who have these expressive ways happen to be gay in sexual orientation, but not all.

By the same token, there are many homosexuals who have *no traditionally feminine mannerisms*. Traditional 'signs" of masculinity are blurring or becoming more complex. Even a cowboy hat and a flannel shirt are no guarantee - see the movie *Brokeback Mountain* - nor is Republican leanings or living in Idaho credentials enough to make you a "Man's Man"- see Senator Larry Craig. Oh, and what is a metro-sexual male? Popular culture defines him as a heterosexual with style and fashion sense. Gone are marriages referred to as "velvet" or "New York Marriages" that hid the homosexuality of celebrities. Only in recent times has the idea of "coming out of the closet" even been an option. Certainly, we no longer live in Mayberry RFD or Beaver Cleaver's neighborhood.

For lesbians there is the stereotype shorthaired woman who has forgone feminine clothing for more traditionally masculine garb, AND conversely, there are many heterosexual women who find short hair their style. In addition, there are certainly many non-lesbian women who find the ridiculous pressure and expense of fashion a waste of time and resources. Add to this generalized lack of clear, perceivable identifiers the complication that some people stray from one sexual preference to another *during their lifetimes* - see Anne Heche or Elton John among many others. Again, clear roles are fuzzier now than in the more-prescribed past.

Several people claim that they have very powerful "gaydar"- a supposed ability to sense if someone is gay - male or female. Some declare they are so accurate with their "gaydar" that they can tell who is gay even if the person in question is conscious of it or not. Valid or not, "gaydar" may be often inaccurate simply because circumscribed gender behavior patterns are just less common.

What we need to face is that - whatever our personal feelings about a student's lifestyle preferences - we need to accept their presence and serve them equally. We cannot only love Christians or people of our own nationality, political leanings or sexual orientation for that matter. We cannot pick and choose because that is not America. Just as we must serve and lead people of different cultures and students that just seem strange to us, we must do our job for all students regardless of their sexual orientation. We have to accept kids for who they are, and then do all we can to make them the best beings they can be in the time we have together.

Given all the curricular and assessment pressures that keep a teacher's life ablaze, we just have to avoid the foolish consideration of converting someone religiously or attempting to re-direct someone's deep seated sexual preference. We do not have the time even if it were possible. My godson, who happens to be gay, has faced a gauntlet of attempts to make him heterosexual. His favorite question from these well meaning and irritating people is: "how can you be sure you're not straight if you've never had sex with a woman?" His response is clear and simple, 'I'll try straight if you try gay- remember, you can't be sure until you try it." He should not have to face this gauntlet.

A school in Southern California is a case study in gender relations within the school and in the school's community. A teacher named Kurt Dearie, who happens to be a happily married heterosexual as well as a highly regarded staff developer for the national AVID program was asked by some students to be the advisor to the first Gay Straight Alliance Club at his school. His story and the stories of his students are inspiring and illustrative of the plight of gay students in our public schools. In Mr. Dearie's words:

"My High School's Gay Straight Alliance Club (GSA) was founded by five students in 2003 with the purpose of making schools safe and ending harassment and discrimination of lesbian and gay students. Met by hostility from school board members, administrators, teachers, staff, and the community, these students began to strategize how they were going to bring about change. Among their ideas was to reach out to staff and educate them regarding the issues gay students face and what staff could do to make school safe for all students. The GSA club continues to conduct training working shops for educators and was created by them in order to share specific things that can be done to help make schools safe. I also have attached one student's story that was shared with teachers during one of our workshops. He asked the teachers in the room why he should go on living if he "was going to be hated every day of his life?" The room was silent, and then people began to cry. No one could offer him an answer. Carlos' story is just one of the many that I hear each year and the tens of thousands that remain untold by children across this country. There is a Carlos in every one of our classes and I believe as educators we have a moral obligation to act. Elie Weisel, Auschwitz survivor and author of the book *Night* was right when he said, "Take sides. Neutrality helps the oppressor, never the victim. Silence encourages the tormentor, never the tormented." I have spent lunch eating pizza with the students of the GSA club every Wednesday for the past 7 years, and I marvel at the change in the school culture that they have brought about. There are now GSA clubs in over 20 states and change is possible, but more educators must act, they must be willing to take a stand and confront the harassment and discrimination that is plaguing our schools."

Here is a story of one of Kurt's students:

"I am a 14 year-old student at this high school. I like magic, skating, and having fun. I am part of the Gay Straight Alliance Club and we are the voice for all homosexual people. We want people to understand the risks gay students face because of society's treatment them. Today in schools students are always saying, "That's so gay, or you're a "faggot". Using these terms or allowing them to be used is not just discriminating against a whole group of people you are also hurting the feelings and destroying their self-esteem as well. There are people all around you that are gay but act like everyone else. Just because they don't act differently doesn't mean they aren't offended or hurt by the things they hear. As we said earlier, the risks of suicide are four times greater than normal heterosexuals. The reason young people do this is because they feel isolated and hated by everyone around them. This subject is very personal to me. I've wondered if it is really worth living if I am going to be hated every day of my life. Stuff like this doesn't just happen in high school either. It starts as early as elementary school. When I was in middle school people would walk up to me just to call me "faggot". It hurt! The worst part is that no one did anything about it. If you would just tell students that saying these things are unacceptable ñ even things like "that's gay". It would help a lot. If you don't stop these things from being said, there will only be more prejudice, more hate, more isolation and more unnecessary deaths. If it doesn't stop, it may eventually be one of your students that end up like the king of hearts ñ the one they call the suicide king."

Again, the greatest challenge and difficulty to teaching is ministering to those students who make us uncomfortable. For some educators, the student with the Mohawk hairdo or studded armbands is difficult. For others, a student of a different race or culture or very quiet introverts may make us uncomfortable. There are all manner of students with all manner of life stories and teaching them all is VERY hard. Yet, this is our charge, our task. Acceptance and forgiveness is the key to lasting in such a vocation.

Sexual Desire in the Classroom

To what extent is sex occurring in the classroom and in the hall every day on every campus across this nation? Well interestingly, most of the sex occurs only in the minds and thoughts of students and teachers. President Jimmy Carter stated famously in his 1976 "Playboy" interview "I've looked on many women with lust. I've committed adultery in my heart many times. God knows I will do this and forgives me."

Teachers, administrators, secretaries, custodians, gardeners, coaches, guest speakers and students, all have intermittent thoughts of sex in their heads. They are involuntary – part of our physiology and millions of years of natural selection. The people involved are probably not immediately conscious of this reality. However, their amygdalas are reacting to visual and auditory and sometimes tactile stimuli. Can you imagine the scandal if the "truth-telling" FMRI were to be strapped to any of us and we were shown images of some "well developed" pubescent girl or boy students?" Anyone could see the increased Amygdala reactivity and know that our brain is being excited by what our eyes are seeing. Remember the functional MRI is capable of detecting minute changes in activity in specific locations of the brain, and the Amygdala is highly reactive to sexual sensory input.

Technology and neuroscience have advanced to the point where our inner, even pre-conscious urges and feelings can be exposed and observed. Yet our society -- with its puritanical roots -- still avoids looking at a rather GIGANTIC elephant in the classroom. From newspapers to electronic media, sex scandals between teachers and students have been called "epidemic." A recent flurry of cases in Florida has drawn attention to female teachers and their pubescent male students.

A testament to prurient interests in us all, women perpetrators quickly become the objects of voyeuristic media "tsk-tsking" and an extreme amount of attention – as least attractive female perpetrators do. The media will follow these stories for as long as they are able. Sex sells newspapers and magazines and TV shows. However a 2004 Federal Department of Education study - the only exhaustive study on teacher misconduct - reported that 10 % of the roughly 50 million American students experience inappropriate sexual conduct by school employees. The study also found that males were responsible for 90% of the improprieties.

As to whether these cases are increasing it is difficult to tell. In the '50s -- and even the sexually "free" '60s -- various veils of secrecy still existed and in order to avoid scandal and insults to a school's reputation, incidents were "swept under the rug." Just like the Catholic Church's litany of sex scandals, the perpetrators were more protected in past times – perhaps, as a consequence of our hush-hush Puritanism.

Matthew Felling, media director for the Center of Media and public affairs offered "The story is part crime drama, part penthouse letter." Basically, the media and the public like the drama and salacious details from these sad situations. He went on to say that "It all began with the Letourneau case, which was a gateway drug for the news networks. They got hooked on it." What was once hidden from view or swept under the rug for all the wrong reasons is now known by all for all the wrong reasons: our creepy curiosity with things salacious and the media's readiness to sell it to us.

Considering the fact that there is a demonstrated problem today with sexual predation in schools – as in most other segments of society -- the real question isn't about the sensational nature of these cases or whether our society is crumbling like Rome's. What we need to face is that humans are sexual beings – some might say hyper-sexual beings when compared to other mammalian species -- and nowhere is that truer than among adolescents coming into their first sexual "heat" in middle and high school.

We can't know for sure whether this phenomenon is worsening or just being better publicized, but what we do know is that sexual drive has been a powerful emotion and driving force in human beings for all time. So the focus needs to remain, not on sensationalism, nor hand-wringing, but rather real, honest and focused remedies. One barrier to effectively deal with this issue is our cultural schizophrenia and general discomfort with sex. Vapid popular indulgences like "Sex In the City" are over-kill precisely because the collective us prefers the wink-wink, nod-nod sexual innuendo to straight talk about sex. We love the double entendre.

We recently experienced four high-profile cases of sexual misconduct over a two-year period at a charter high school in San Diego. The District responded by threatening to revoke the high school's charter and by forcing school personnel to attend a district-created training. I happened to have experienced that training. In the district administrator's Power Point presentation was a slide entitled; "Appropriate Behaviors" and, under this title were several bulleted items such as "kissing," "fondling," "inappropriate hugging," "stroking" etc. I was understandably confused, so I raised my hand to ask about it. Keep in mind that the room was anxiously silent at the time with 120+ staff members staring at the same bizarre slide of "Appropriate Behaviors." The district administrator called on me, and I said, "I must have missed something, but why is there a list of inappropriate behaviors listed bellow a slide titled: "Appropriate Behaviors"? Without pausing, he stated, "I'm attempting to create a false-dichotomy." He was attempting to create a complex contrast between what "acceptable" and "unacceptable" behavior are by mislabeling the slide we were viewing. This is just bad presenting. Leaving a very important point unclear and unstated is just ridiculous. The district representative had a sophisticated vocabulary but little knowledge of clear presentation or teaching skills. Because of the insidious nature of sexual urges, direct and confrontative techniques need to be utilized. So not only was the presentation poorly designed, it may have actually sent a subliminal message that bad behavior was okay.

I was stunned. I got his point, but I know that too many of my fellow faculty members did not. In addition, for all the passive listeners that were somewhat detached, this slide was actually giving a subtle nudge towards "inappropriate behaviors." This is because, when you are not critically involved with any presentation of information like this ridiculous training or even the run-of-the-mill TV commercial, the subliminal effect on our brains can be enormous. Advertisers know this. Several cans of "Green Giant" vegetables are bought almost in trance states by shoppers precisely because they were passively soaking up Green Giant's catchy tune. Advertisers have called it "subliminal seduction," and there is a book detailing what advertisers know about this tricky sub-conscious strategy to manipulate your mind and behaviors.

Have you ever heard of trainings on this topic using direct and clear language, like, "Do NOT HAVE SEX or MANIPULATE SEXUAL feelings in any of your students?" This DOES need to be said, right? Why don't we say it? Is it because it's too obvious? No, I think not. It's because we are too uncomfortable with the subject matter that we don't say it; and, this ironically weakens the message and the moral purpose needed to stem the inappropriate behavior. Simply stated, we need to face and accept that sex is here and is powerful. We need a present, relevant and equally strong clear response: "DON'T HAVE SEX WITH STUDENTS!" This sharp clarity will do much to cut through our puritanical cultural fog. Hopefully, this will spark the burner of continued clear and direct talk about an issue which will not go away without transparent truth talking.

Next on the agenda, it's important to clarify why having sex with adolescents is a bad idea. Developmentally, teens are in a "perfect storm" of socio-sexual-emotional evolution. They are negotiating new physical and emotional territory with pubescent bodies, acne; odd voice modulation; new hair growth in new areas: arms, legs, knees and elbows that can grow at varying speeds with varying amounts of pain. In addition, their brains are undergoing similarly complex growth challenges.

First, their PFCs - pre-frontal cortices - are forming quickly but not quickly enough to offset the influence of the new growth in the primitive brain, especially the Amygdala. At around the age of 14, the Amygdala begins growing. That sends its female owners on an emotional roller coaster and boys on a quest to break bones and assert their authority and challenge the limits of their physical bodies. Too many girls also engage in sexual risk-taking and begin experiencing weakened self-perceptions at the same time. Also, both boys and girls suffer the cascade of several new hormones in their blood which affects feelings and cognitive social interactions to name a few.

Indeed, the desire to 'fit-in" or accede to peer pressure is one of the new tests "hormonally handed" to teens. This one burden itself causes several levels of challenge and awkwardness. Kids who were once confident and self possessed suddenly face a new distracting desire to "join the tribe." Add new sexual urges and you have the potential of a multi-faceted nightmare where once calm children become 'live wires" who experience bouts of anxiety, depression and anger they never experienced before.

Add to this the common disassociation with their parents that teens experience and a new layer of vulnerability visits them. As a result, they will often look to their adult relationships at school for the emotional intimacy, which has diminished in their parental relationship. Teachers can become a student's new parental replacement. Toss dramatically stronger sexual urges into this mix and you have the "clear and present danger" of a sexual encounter.

The deep irony of a teen's sex and emotional intimacy are revealed when the adult succumbs to the "baser" of these two needs. Generally, the injury to trust and emotional security -- the hallmarks of true mentorship -- caused by these inappropriate sexual unions is long and deep in the victim child. Injuries to those very mentor relationships cause scars, which take years to heal, if they ever do. Thus, the ugliness of these unions is that they exploit the teen's elevated need for a stable, secure mentor - one solid "mirror" of calm.

The trust and emotional security that victims seek in these dangerous unions, horribly leads to the complete obliteration of the trust and mentor connection. Sex is far more complex and multi-dimensional than the physical act. It yanks the child out of the security of childhood and protected relationships they have so-far enjoyed with adults. It makes them adult peers, forcing them into an unfamiliar new role before they are emotionally ready. It destroys the stability of their world, creates a new obligation and a new expectation of closeness and support. When, in the majority of cases, that relationship doesn't materialize, it intensifies the child/adult schizophrenia already a part of the teen transition. It sends the kid into a desert of alienation and insecurity at a time when they are least capable of handling it; and, inevitably leads to a mistrust of future mentors and, often, hurtful sexual hang-ups.

For adult school employees who perpetrate these crimes – and, make no mistake, they are nothing short of criminal -- there are also long-lasting negative consequences. When caught with sufficient evidence, these individuals will and should lose their jobs, future prospects, and the respect of their peers. Many lose or severely damage familial and spousal relationships – and, sometimes, even those with their own offspring. They also get arrested and go to jail. They too suffer emotional difficulty and negative social consequences for years after the sex is but a brief, preternatural memory.

Thus, it is important that the school employees know explicitly the consequences for the child, but also for themselves if they engage sexually with students. What is important to know is that regardless of age, humans can be remarkably child-like in behavior given the 'right" circumstances. Drug and alcohol influence may cause enough of a lapse of conscious thoughtfulness whereby adult-child sex may occur. In an article in "O" the Oprah magazine, female perpetrators of these crimes are not pedophiles because "what leads to their downfall is emotional immaturity." ("O" July 15, 2008)

Some adults have an unfulfilled emotional need for various psychological or personal reasons which given the "right" situation, overcome their consciousness and result in sex acts. This is also the case for male teachers, often seen as the more predatory of the genders. Over the 23 years of my teaching, I have witnessed occasions where men, men very senior to their students in years, emotionally "fall" for a female student.

Obviously, it's far easier to become indignant at the more predatory malefactors. Yet, these less predatory or "emotional" cases are no less undesirable as they erode the necessary bond of trust between children, their parents and school employees. While they must be aired and their origins understood, stories of teacher misconduct are, nonetheless, like a cancer that eats away at the collegiality that is already difficult to achieve in the classroom, but is so necessary if children are going to be receptive to learning.

We have them for such a short time; and it is already difficult to reach across the demographic divide between teen and adult – it can take a whole term to accomplish. To plant a seed of suspicion that a teacher could be a predator pretty much blocks any progress; and undermines the hard work and sacrifice of the vast majority of teachers who care about their charges and make sacrifices for them year after year.

Jesus said: "But if anyone causes one of these little ones who believe in me to sin, it would be better for him to have a large millstone hung around his neck and to be drowned in the depths of the sea."

Jesus was a very forgiving guy. In the context of the damage that can be done a child, we can't really afford any degree of laxity in this area. Sex crimes are incremental and progressive and can be a very difficult habit to break. As for the predatory few who may, at some point, go over the line with a student, it can't be swept under the carpet. Many of the cases of "creepy" teachers with whom I am familiar -- mostly males -- are either "unconscious" or barely conscious of their inappropriate attention toward a student. It's an easy mistake to make. Human beings of all ages and both sexes get these feelings; they're part of our humanity. The trap is to not recognize when these feelings are bubbling up – or worse, nurture them. There is a line that should not be crossed; and, to ensure that it isn't, there are patterns of behavior and attitudes that need to be rolled far back. But the creepy teacher does not consciously analyze his feelings – either because he is not aware of where the line is or because he willingly suppresses his super-ego -- the check on his own thinking and behavior. By letting himself get lost in these kinds of thoughts, he becomes less capable of self-correction or impulse modulation.

It can start absent-mindedly. Students have, on occasion, come to me complaining about a teacher who "touches me unnecessarily," or "stares at my breasts, not my eyes," or "stares at me from across the room." Even young girls can sense sexual interest and differentiate between attention that is appropriate and that which is not. Not all males have the same degree of awareness of the subtleties of these interactions. The male authority figure or role model is a very important one in a young girl's life, starting with the special relationship that, ideally, girls have with their fathers. Just as boys have a special relationship with mothers who are their first source of nurturing and approval, the father/authoritarian figure plays a different, but equally important, role for their daughters. In an ideal world, fathers are responsible for passing on morals and values to their daughters from an early age. The father has the primary mission of protecting his children – boys and girls -- from all manner of threats, while supporting their aspirations. It's been observed that girls often marry boys with the same characteristics as their fathers which is, perhaps, as it should be. It is only natural that the young girl will seek approval and attention from other older males in similar roles. The onus to control the situation is on the adult male – ALWAYS--because in the real world, we often see students without a sufficiently supportive home life. These children, both boys and girls, are particularly vulnerable to the older predator. This is one of those situations where the educator cannot even afford THE APPEARANCE OF IMPROPRIETY.

For these children, the teacher-student relationship can be a conflicted one. Young girls are, oftentimes, more alert to a teacher's attentions and the relationship than is the male teacher who interacts with many students at a rapid pace all day long and who is the approval giver, not the approval seeker. The student is more likely to recognize attention that carries both approval and a vague undercurrent of threat than the inattentive adult male. I call these "dumb" signs or unconscious expressions of desire – glances, smiles, unwarranted pats on the shoulder, excessive attention that just sort of "leak thru" during student-teacher interactions.

"Leak thru" signs of desire happen precisely because the male is unaware of what he's doing. He is truly dumb to how the student perceives his attention. I have told male teachers about how some of their students have noticed that they place all the buxom teens in the front row, and have been met with disbelieving stares and responses of "Huh?" "Really?"

So, repeated straight talk about how sensitive and perceptive girls are is in order. Teachers also need to understand how emotionally vulnerable they are and the confusion that arises out of a sexuality that is "in flux". It would help to get all school employees on the "same bus" as to what is best behavior with our young charges. Perhaps, panels of students discussing honest perceptions about this area of sex in the classroom would help. We need to hear the unheard voices of the most important people in this challenging aspect of school life: the kids themselves.

Several female students of mine over the years, especially my AVID students who I get to know much more because of the family atmosphere built into the AVID elective class, have shared their trials and tribulations with male teachers who suffer from "leak thru." They shared that they become quite adept at detecting the creep even from its most subtle beginnings, the most fleeting, furtive glances as well, of course, as the ridiculous and blatant.

After graduating, one girl complained to me of a teacher who would hold his hands out in front of himself, palms facing her as if he was preparing to fondle her breasts. She told me he would make small gestures with his fingers while he talked, all the while keeping his hands in the general "fondling" location. This weird form of "leak thru" troubled her mightily, however, she felt that she couldn't say anything about it because it never became overt. It just didn't seem to rise to clear misbehavior. It made her anxious and uncomfortable, but she didn't think that his actions were quite blatant enough that a formal complaint would be given credibility by the administration.

What the male teachers, and a growing number of female teachers, need to face is that students between 14 and 19 are often very attractive. Their bodies, hormones and beings are naturally growing and developing sexually at a rapid pace; and, for most of human history, these were peak reproductive years. That's the physiological aspect. But society has changed and our culture is sufficiently complex that children need to be protected and nurtured for a much longer period of time. They may appear mature, but they are not mature. They are not capable of giving informed consent; and the inevitable bad outcomes from these relationships represent betrayals of trust that can have a long-lasting impact on the child.

Yes, they are pretty or handsome, BUT you cannot touch them, nor ought you lead them on towards the romantic feelings for the sake of your own ego gratification. Conscious awareness is again key. Although it seems a bit ridiculous to state the obvious, the sexual drive in all of us is so powerful and pervasive that the brain needs to be frequently reminded to keep us from slipping into inappropriate behavior. Rather than hoping this issue will go away, we need to be as transparent as we can. We need to be frank and clear, almost like a vow or promise. It will help cut through the foggy world where "one thing leads to another."

For Further Exploration

Gender, Sexual Orientation and Sexual Desire and the Classroom

Publications:

Brizendine, L. (2006). *The female brain.* New York, NY: Broadway Books. [This book follows the development of woman's brains from infancy through teen years, adulthood and menopause.]

Brizendine, L. (2010). *The male brain.* New York, NY: Broadway Books. [This book brings the latest in stae of the art science to help us understand the male brain.]

Lipkin, A. (2003). Beyond diversity day: A q&a on gay and lesbian issues in schools (curriculum, cultures, and (homo)sexualities). New York, NY: Rowman and Littlefield.
[This book respectfully discusses issues specific to Gay and Lesbian students.]

Martino, W., Kehler, M., & Weaver-Hightower, M. (2009). *The problem with boys' education: Beyond the backlash.* New York, NY: Routledge.
[This book is a collection of essays focused on the challenges of maximizing male learning.]

Websites:

EthicsEd. (2009). *National issues, local solutions.* Retrieved from http://www.ethicsed.com/sesame-inc
[This has information about preventing and responding to sexual misconduct in schools.]

GSA Network. (2009). *Gay-Straight Alliance Network.* Retrieved from http://gsanetwork.org/
[This has information on Gay and Lesbian issues.]

The Mid-Atlantic Equity Consortium, Inc.. (1993). *Beyond Title IX: Gender equity issues in schools*. Retrieved from http://www.maec.org/pdf/beyondIX.pdf
[This is a discussion of research data and theory regarding gender equity in American education.]

6

Resilience and Hidden Gifts

"Everything great in the world comes from neurotics. They alone have founded our religions and composed our masterpieces."

-**Marcel Proust** 1902

"The biggest mistake of past centuries in teaching has been to treat all children as if they were variants of the same individual, and thus to feel justified in teaching them the same subjects in the same ways."

- Howard Gardner 1994

Andrew stayed after class, staring straight ahead with a lost expression on his face in the first class I taught during my first year. Realizing he was at the least, distracted, I asked him if he was ok. He looked up at me and said, "My dad tried to kill me and my sister last night." I froze; my brain froze. I remember the frustrated feeling of rushing around in my head in vain for anything to say or do. Nothing came. Finally I managed to ask, "What do you mean? "What happened?

He managed to say that his dad had just gone crazy and that he became inexplicably violent and had it not been for neighbors and friends, the outcome would have been much worse. He and I stayed in touch in a mentor, mentee manner for years. It wasn't until ten years later that he came clean about the details of that night, primarily because he said he just couldn't face the savagery and fear of that night when he was only fifteen and his honored role model slipped into what was later diagnosed as a form of Schizophrenia. Suffice it to say, what he and his sister experienced was indeed horrifying and degrading.

The beauty and miracle of Andrew's true story is the power of mentorship and the healing power of resiliency. Although I was instrumental in part for guiding him at the time and for a few years after the tragic and horrific event, today, Andrew is at his best. He is now married, has a son by a previous marriage and is thriving. His current wife Olivia has also supported and loved him to even further health. The key is that Olivia and I lived a commitment to Andrew and accepted his occasional stumblings. Andrew also has confessed that that there have been other mentors along the way, even a teacher who only knew him a short while had a profound and lasting effect on his beliefs about himself. The result is a man of incredible depth, discipline, creativity and focus that I rarely see in anyone.

This was not true of Andrew throughout the intervening years since his trauma. The key is that his miracle or demonstrated resiliency is real and palpable now. To those who first meet him now, he seems a prodigy, but those who have known him know his has been a tough road. Now, occasionally, Andrew turns the tables and becomes quite a wise advisor to me. This is the miracle of influence one can have as an educator, and it is grounded in the human heart and the innate toughness and redeem-ability of the spirit.

A great revolution is taking place in American psychology, probably the most revolutionary development in its history. This movement is called the "Resiliency" revolution. Central to the message of resiliency is the concept that we all require stress and challenge in order to fully develop our talents, grow intellectually and spiritually and become healthier beings. Another important element to resiliency is the perception that what were once considered "deficits" -- like Attention Deficit Hyperactive Disorder (ADHD) or even depression -- are now being understood as having some hidden benefits as well.

As Dr. Larry Brendtro observes in his book *The Resilience Revolution,* "During much of the 20th century, psychology was preoccupied with pathology, and tomes were written about anger, guilt, depression, and anxiety. But after decades dwelling on the dark side of human behavior, a psychology of human strength is emerging."

Psychologists are beginning to look and find the hidden gifts embedded in what they once identified only as pathologies in the fully negative sense of the term. For example, it has been estimated that ADHD has been a genetic condition for more than 50,000 years. Therefore as a condition, it must have had some survival benefits for early human – obvious ones being a hyper awareness of the environment, an advanced ability to multi-task and higher energy levels. If you were a teen running through the bush in Africa 50,000 years ago – or even if you were a teen running through the forests of Colonial America – these traits had obvious advantages. But if you are a teen in a 21st Century middle or high school consigned to sitting in a chair all day long, not so much.

Hyperactivity still has challenges associated with it, but because of the environment in which it occurs rather than some assumed pathology in the teens who exhibit it. Now, with a few years of retrospective, we have observed that many of these high-energy teens go on to become successful high-energy adults once they are no longer consigned to classroom desks and free to apply their talents to occupational challenges. Very few human tendencies can be automatically labeled as negative —although, some may be situationally inappropriate. As educators, we would do well to take a longer perspective and look at the whole student with new eyes that seek to find each of our student's hidden gifts.

Depression is another challenge to which students are often susceptible. Its universally negative context also is being re-examined. One corollary to depression is that individuals who experience it usually also have greater sensitivity to the people and world around them. Those who suffer from bouts of black feel more. They perceive the world more acutely in the affective or emotional domain. That is not to say that the suffering of those with depression is in any way diminished by this realization. What it does suggest is that there is a greater, fuller meaning to the condition than that which only labeled it a deficit. Some of those who have suffered from depression have turned out to be some of our greatest artists, authors and leaders – Vincent Van Gogh and Silvia Plath, for example.

We should now endeavor to more fully examine many psychological conditions with a view toward weighing their benefits as well as liabilities. We actually will begin to see others who are challenging these assumptions in light of new possibilities. Most importantly, educators need to know and be aware of their own stereotypes and reactions to ADHD and depression. Classrooms are rife with regular doses of tragedy because of challenges such as divorces, deaths of family members or beloved pets, drug problems and many other ups and downs that are a part of life. As Desmund Tutu archbishop of South Africa and advisor to Nelson Mandela so rightly states, "We must look on children in need not as problems but as individuals with potential to share if they are given the opportunity. Even when they are really troublesome, there is some good in them, for; after all, they were created by God. I would hope we could find creative ways to draw out of our children the good that is there in each of them." Seeing this way is clearly challenging, yet the benefits of this more optimistic and empowering philosophy are hard to deny.

David Dobbs in his article in *The Atlantic,* entitled *The Science of Success,* creates a metaphor for understanding this new way of "seeing" people. He identifies people as Dandelions and Orchids. Dandelions are people who seem to thrive anywhere without much nourishment under a wide range of environments like you see in fields. Orchids are those among us who may be more delicate in nature and in need of more specific attention in order to nurture them and bring them to their full potential. They are delicate, but in the right environment and under the right care, they can blossom into beings that are quite beautiful and remarkable. Dobbs goes on to say that, "About a quarter of all human beings carry the best-documented gene variant for depression, while more than a fifth carry the variant . . . which is associated with externalizing, antisocial, and violent behaviors, as well as ADHD, anxiety, and depression."

In a sense "difficult people are everywhere – and, apparently, that is just how nature intended it. This means that nearly half of all humans are susceptible to experiencing some form of depression, ADHD or anxiety disorder during their lifetimes. We can no longer label these people as deficient and dismiss their potential for growth. As educators we have to find ways, as Archbishop Tutu recommended, to grow the greatness in each individual as best we can. It seems that Dandelions are ordinary and Orchids are extraordinary.

Consider individuals like Ozzy Osborne of rock and roll fame. He entertained millions, created a niche for heavy metal music and wrote some remarkable tunes. He was also eccentric and nearly killed himself with drugs and alcohol. As strange as he may seem to many of us, he also had great gifts. Also consider the two titans of American technology, Bill Gates and Steve Jobs. Both are college dropouts. Gates left college because Harvard was not interesting enough. Jobs dropped out for similar reasons; and, as brilliant as he is, he is also known as a person who can be hard to work for. Both have gifts and liabilities and both needed the right environment to do their great work – both are classic orchids. As Dobbs notes in his article, "Yes, this new thinking goes, these bad genes can create dysfunction in unfavorable contexts - but they can also enhance function in favorable contexts."

Dr. Jay Belsky of the University of London describes this new thinking this way, "Most . . . Mental-illness researchers . . . focus on vulnerability. They don't see the upside, because they don't look for it. It's like dropping a dollar bill beneath a table. You look under the table, you see the dollar bill, and you grab it. But you completely miss the five that's just beyond your feet."

So again, the idea is that we start to really "see" students and co-workers in a different light – to look beyond the obvious to see their potential gifts and capacities. Consider the American artist Andy Warhol who coined the phrase "Fifteen minutes of fame" and made Campbell soup cans pop art icons. He was a rare and talented man and thinker, and he also suffered from extreme social anxiety. At parties he would suddenly disappear, and was once found hiding under a table to escape the anxiety he felt around people. Winston Churchill is another orchid, a great man who led Britain through one of its darkest historical hours. He was universally disliked for his personality and toughness; and that is why immediately after the war he was ushered out of power. He had great skills and powers during wartime, but he was very challenging to deal with as well.

Seeing other humans with this new consciousness of positive potential will be challenging because our brains like to label and pigeonhole both things and people. It's a survival technique for dealing with a world of excessive stimuli. We like labels because they make life easier. Labeling someone as a "hyper" child is just plain easier than the hard work of dealing with that characteristic. But applying a label to the child also puts him on the metaphorical shelf, removes him from the mainstream and almost predisposes him to failure. As the authors Robert Rosenthal and Lenore Jacobson wrote in their book, *Pygmalion in the Classroom,* "Simply put, when teachers expect students to do well and show intellectual growth, they do; when teachers do not have such expectations, performance and growth are not so encouraged and may in fact be discouraged in a variety of ways."

We need to take the trouble to look for the greatness in every student, even when it's wrapped in behavioral problems and has not yet unfolded to full flower. However, there is great difficulty seeing everyone as evolving beings with potential. Robert Irwin, a California conceptual artist whose work can be found at the Getty Museum near Los Angeles and at the University of California campus at San Diego, understands the problem with labeling or objectifying anything. In fact he wrote a book with a rather poignant title: *Seeing is Forgetting the Name of the Thing One Sees.* When we label a complex human being, we are not open to being surprised or having them surpass our label; and so, cannot fully educate them. Once you label something, your brain perceives the "named" qualities far more than those which are hidden, and is reluctant "see" beyond the new label.

Your belief in their as-yet unfulfilled capacities are diminished and this further results in how hard you try. Even your body language will signal your limited view of the child in question. Education is all about growth, hope and positive change, not about defining a static condition or trait. Because we are human and labeling is an eons-old function of the discriminating faculty in our brains, labeling may be permissible in our private lives. But when we enter an educational environment we need a different discipline and a greater awareness. We have a much higher commission to put aside what is easy or convenient for ourselves for the sake of the children in our charge. This is our moral purpose, and that is what should inform all of our actions and behavior, conscious or unconscious. We have to be mindful and aware of our inner lives as much as possible, so we do not project messages to our students that they are lass capable or without hope. Dr. Brendtro agrees that, "Those who fail to see strengths and potentials in troubled youth will always believe coercion is essential and empowerment naive."

The way we treat people can even affect their genes. Called "epigenetics" the idea is that the environment affects the expression or non-expression of certain genes. A new understanding in genetics, this too has radical implications. The way you treat and interact with learners affects how their genes create who they are – especially among young people whose physical and emotional profiles are still forming. The belief that genes are fixed and inert to environment has been overthrown. Several twins were followed after adoption and foster care, and those who had bad experiences were compared to their brothers or sisters who had healthy experiences. Their genes were very differently expressed, and the behaviors and attitudes of these twins were very different.

Dr. Richard Tremblay from the University of Montreal has studied this phenomenon and has stated, "Mother rats that lick and groom their children positively affect the expression of certain genes through the increase of serotonin; it causes the fuller expression of more genes." People and all other mammals are equally impressionable.

We have to be more right brained in regards to education in America to fully understand resiliency and hidden gifts. The left-brain loves to create boundaries, objectify and label reality. While all these functions serve a purpose, within the work of learning and mentoring they can be dangerous. We have to have a different consciousness in the classroom and on the playground. The problem lies in the fact that most of American education is mired in left-brained capacities:

*We standardize testing and curriculum design

*We often ask, "Is it measurable?"

*We place subject areas in hierarchies of importance

*We categorize and label children as special ed., remedial, college prep, EL, ADHD, etc

*We give grades

*We often believe "what we do" is more important than "who we are"

As the neural-anatomist and stroke survivor Dr. Jill Bolte-Taylor has noted in her book *My Stroke of Insight*, "One of the natural functions of my right mind is to bring me new insight in this moment so I can update old files that contain outdated information. Many of us make judgments with our left hemisphere and then are not willing to step to the right for a file update."

American education desperately needs a "file update." We need this shift in curriculum design because we need to engage our students in more active, problem solving and social learning; we need this shift in how we "see" students and learners because their capacities and gifts are complex and ever-changing; we need this because we need to see that this work is human and people- focused and not something easily "standardized." We have tunnel vision because of this standardized testing. It rarely assesses the creativity and problem-solving that we need in America now.

Consider the popular example of standardization in the world of food: Chicken McNuggets. They are the same in London and Shanghai, Los Angeles and Mexico City. You can count on them, and they are horrible food. Yes, reliable and remarkably standardized and very unhealthy. Dr. Robinson says we become "enthralled" by the reality that surrounds us and accept it with little question. Standardized, factoid tests are so much the norm, we just live with them. Well, he sees this as dangerous to growth and creativity, "One of the enemies of creativity and innovation, especially in relation to our own development, is common sense . . . As soon as something seems the most obvious thing in the world, it means we have abandoned all attempts at understanding it."

There are more authentic ways of assessing kids like effort and improvement. We can learn so much more about a student's character by how much he improves and grows than when we just check if he has the right answer. Many progressive educators know that the most primal element in motivation is in fact the pride of improvement or accomplishment that the student experiences, not their grades.

This is the approach that most Special Education teachers take with their students. They trouble over the challenges an individual student has, and then attempt to communicate this to their primary teachers and parents who care for and teach the child. Then they reassess whether the approach is working and re-communicate the new ideas with all stakeholders through the whole process of trying to educate the child. They do this often with students who have extreme challenges, be they physical, emotional or cognitive. This is the ideal approach to each child. It is the ultimate method; and, unfortunately, it is impossible for the standard classroom teacher. The model CAN still be an inspiration to all teachers, though, because trying against great odds and against the challenges and bad habits that students often harbor is our job. Also, we do not face and live this challenge just for the benefits that accrue to the child, but also for the transformation it allows we educators to experience as well.

Larry Brendtro describes this loop of influence from student to teacher in his book *Deep Brain Learning,* "While personal traits are important, behavior is always a *reciprocal transaction* with others, not a solo performance. A parent influences a child, but the child also influences the parent. The teacher impacts the student, but the student also has an effect on teacher behavior. Children select their peers which often become their significant others and in turn are influenced by them. We live in reciprocity, joining together in a hymn of harmony or in a dance of disturbance."

We are not just the sum of traits or static conditions. This is core to the success of the national AVID program, which has demonstrably improved college success in student populations identified as "under-represented" on university campuses. Key to their program is a teacher who devotes him/herself to the student's ambitions and mentors them to attain them. Besides AVID's curriculum of research-based best-practices, the AVID class is a family of students that creates a very positive peer group atmosphere which develops a sense of hope for personal achievement gained through hard work and determination.

In his article *Resilience: It's Academic,* Rob Gira, Executive Vice President of the national AVID program discusses why Resilience Theory is important for teachers and mentors in the online AVID publication, *ACCESS,* "resilience is an interactive phenomenon, not distinctly related to genetics and that a child's interaction with the educational environment matters just as much as the child's temperament, IQ, or genes. Thus, . . . a child's resilience is not just dependent on the child alone, but on interactions with others and whether those others provide successful support."

This ability to focus on or discover hidden gifts is important nowhere more than in the realm of Special Education which began in 1975 with the passage of the *Education for All Handicapped Children Act*. Ten years after the act was passed, there were some 4.5 million children identified. Today that number has grown to more than six million. Again, a growing number of children need extra attention paid to "seeing" beyond their deficits to their uniqueness and potential. The point is that no matter whom we are or how old, we are able to improve ourselves, given the right environment and support. Science has photographed new cells growing in the brain of a 78-year-old man. Recent brain research has clearly demonstrated that our brains – and, thus, our skills, abilities and even parts of our personalities -- are malleable and plastic. This knowledge offers real concrete hope. We need to accept this about our students and ourselves.

This is summed up nicely in a Cherokee parable which can be found on the University of Texas Education website:

An old Cherokee was teaching his grandchildren about life. He said, "A battle is raging inside me...it is a terrible fight between two wolves. One wolf represents fear, anger, envy, sorrow, regret, greed, arrogance, self-pity, guilt, resentment, inferiority, lies, false pride, superiority and ego. The other stands for joy, peace, love, hope, sharing, serenity, humility, kindness, benevolence, friendship, empathy, generosity, truth, compassion and faith."

The old man looked at the children with a firm stare. "This same fight is going on inside you, and inside every other person, too."

They thought about it for a minute, and then one child asked his grandfather, "Which wolf will win?"

The old Cherokee replied: "The one you feed."

For Further Exploration

Resilience and Hidden Gifts

Publications:

Brendtro, L. K., & Larson, S. J. (2006). *The resilience revolution: Discovering strengths in challenging kids.* Bloomington, IN: Solution Tree.
[this book details practical and philosophical approaches for teachers.]

Brendtro, L. K., Mitchell, M. L., & McCall, H. J. (2009). *Deep brain learning: Pathways to potential with challenging youth.* Albion, MI: Starr Commonwealth.
[This book describes structures for approaches to maximize learning.]

Dobbs, D. (2009, December Day). The science of success. *The Atlantic.* Retrieved from http://www.theatlantic.com/magazine/archive/2009/12/the-science-of-success/7761/
[This article inspired by the concept of "resiliency" illustrates the need to see gifts over "deficits" in people.]

Gardner, H. (2006). Multiple intelligences: new horizons in theory and practice (2nd ed.). New York, NY: Basic Books.
[This features the new evidence about brain functioning and individual differences in learning.]

Robinson, K. (2009). *The element: how finding your passion changes everything.* New York City, NY: Penguin Group.
[The author demonstrates the need to discover our passions for our sake and the sake of mankind.]

Taylor, J. B. (2006). *My stroke of insight: A brain scientist's personal journey.* New York, NY: Penguin Group.
[This book describes the recovery of the author's stroke and illustrates the need to integrate right brained processing in all that we do.]

Tomlinson, C. A. (1999). *The differentiated classroom: Responding to the needs of all learners.* Columbus, OH: Merrill/ASCD.
[This book describes how to alter content delivery to meet the needs of various individual learning styles.]

Websites:

Advancement Via Individual Determination. (2010). *AVID- Decades of college dreams.* Retrieved from http://www.avid.org
[Their mission is to close the achievement gap by preparing ALL students for college readiness and success in a global society.]

Moblogic.TV. (2008). *Jill Bolte Taylor, PH.D..* Retrieved from http://www. youtube.com/watch?v=AY38pk2hfWI
[Jill Bolte Taylor talks about her stroke and the nature of the brain.]

University of Texas. (n.d.). Transforming lives through resilience education. Retrieved from http://www.utexas.edu/education/resilience/
[This site contains a wealth of resources on teaching with resilience in mind.]

*Some things to do to increase awareness and understanding of resilience:

A Beautiful Life!

Here Are Some Tips That May Bring You A Beautiful Life!

- *Take a 10-30 minute walk every day and while you walk, smile.*

- *Sit in silence for at least 10 minutes each day.*

- *When you wake up in the morning complete the following statement, "My purpose is to ... today."*

- *Live with the 3 E's... Energy, Enthusiasm, Empathy, and the 3 F's ... Faith, Family, Friends.*

- *Spend more time with people over the age of 70 and under the age of 6.*

- *Dream more while you are awake.*

- *Try to make at least three people smile each day.*

- *Realize that life is a school and you are here to learn, pass all your tests. Problems are simply part of the curriculum that appear and fade away like algebra class but the lessons you learn will last a lifetime.*

- *Smile and laugh more. It will keep the energy vampires away.*

- *Life isn't fair, but it's still good.*

- *Life is too short to waste time hating anyone.*

- *Don't take yourself so seriously. No one else does.*

- *You don't have to win every argument. Agree to disagreements.*

- *Make peace with your past, so it won't mess up the present.*

- *Don't compare your life with others'. You have no idea what their journey is all about.*

- *Burn the candles, use the nice sheets. Don't save it for a special occasion. Today is special.*

- *No one is in charge of your happiness except you.*

- *Forgive everyone for everything.*

- What other people think of you is none of your business.

- Time heals almost everything. Give time, time.

- However good or bad a situation is, it will change.

- Your job won't take care of you when you are sick. Your friends will stay in touch.

- Get rid of anything that isn't useful, beautiful, or joyful.

- The best is yet to come... Believe.

- No matter how you feel, get up, dress up, and show up.

- Do the right thing!

- Call your family often.

- Each night before you go to bed complete the following statements: "I am thankful for..." - "Today I accomplished..."

- Remember that you are too blessed to be stressed.

- Enjoy the ride. Remember that this is not Disney World and you certainly don't want a fast pass. Make the most of it and enjoy the ride.

- Unknown